D1576138

MARKET LEADERSHIP STRATEGIES

FOR SERVICE COMPANIES

𝄘𝄘 AMERICAN **MARKETING** ASSOCIATION

MARKET LEADERSHIP STRATEGIES FOR SERVICE COMPANIES

Creating Growth, Profits, and Customer Loyalty

Craig Terrill and Arthur Middlebrooks

NTC Business Books

NTC/Contemporary Publishing Group

Library of Congress Cataloging-in-Publication Data

Middlebrooks, Arthur.
    Market leadership strategies for service companies : creating
growth, profits, and customer loyalty / Arthur Middlebrooks and
Craig Terrill.
      p. cm.
    Includes index.
    ISBN 0-8442-2441-3
    1. Service industries—Marketing—Management. I. Terrill, Craig.
II. Title.
HD9980.5.M53   1999
658.8—dc21   99-10338
                                             CIP

Interior design by Precision Graphics

Published by NTC Business Books in conjunction with the American Marketing Association
A division of NTC/Contemporary Publishing Group, Inc.
4255 West Touhy Avenue, Lincolnwood (Chicago), Illinois 60712-1975 U.S.A.
Printed in the United States of America
International Standard Book Number: 0-8442-2441-3
00 01 02 03 04 05 LB 19 18 17 16 15 14 13 12 11 10 9 8 7 6 5 4 3 2

TO THE GREATEST MEASURE OF SUCCESS—THE unconditional love shared with my wife, Joanne, my kids, Elyse, Grant, and Jessica, my parents, Alan and Barbara, and my lord, Jesus Christ.

Craig

THIS BOOK IS DEDICATED WITH LOVE TO MY wife, Patty, to my son, Carter, and to my parents, Jeanette and Burton.

Art

CONTENTS

ACKNOWLEDGMENTS

THIS BOOK IS THE RESULT OF MANY INSIGHTS shared by services marketing practitioners, many collaborative hours with colleagues, countless doses of caffeine, and endless amounts of tough encouragement from those closest to the project to "keep going." Many thoughtful people have helped us through the process of writing this book with tremendous expertise on the topic. Without them, this book would still be an eclectic set of notes and white papers scattered across several hard drives. To these people, we owe more than can be captured in a few words. Simply stated, thank you!

During the past decade, we have had the privilege of working with over 100 service organizations on issues of growth, innovation, and market leadership. Those that were or became dominant service market leaders typically did so because of key individuals who were market-driven in their thoughts and deeds. We extracted and imbedded in this book tremendous expertise and knowledge from the following people and would like to acknowledge their contributions:

Mike Albrecht, General Manager of IBM Industry and Consulting Services—Americas
Bob Buford, CEO of Buford Television
Jane Burke, CEO of Endeavor Information Systems
Monica Choca, Director of New Business Development for ComEd
Ed Coppola, Senior Vice President of Macerich Company
Lu Cordova, Business Development for @Home
Jim Davidson, President and CEO of Amadeus, North America
Bill Diffenderffer, CEO of XTRA On-line

ix

Terry Franke, Principal, Sales and Marketing for Hewitt Associates

Dale Gifford, CEO of Hewitt Associates

Tom Herowitz, Senior Vice President of Mail Boxes, Etc.

Sandy House, GreenHouse Communications

Paula Jagemann, CEO of OnlineOfficeSupplies.com

Ken Johnson, President of Metamor Solutions

Joan Julian, VP of Online Services Marketing for Encyclopaedia Britannica

Jim Mellado, CEO of the Willow Creek Association

Tom Nardi, VP of Sales and Marketing for NICOR

Gitesch Ramamurthi, President and COO of CCC Information Systems

John Rodelli, Executive Vice President for Bank of America

Frederick Smith, Chairman, President and CEO of FedEx

Bob Waldrop, Senior VP of Communications for Reliant Energy

Maribeth Ward, Director of I/S for Ameritech New Media

Dane West, cofounder of Didax

Bill Zimmermann, CFO of the American Medical Association

In addition to practitioners, we have had the distinct pleasure of engaging with hundreds of MBA students through our classes on the Marketing of Service Organizations at Northwestern's Kellogg Graduate School of Management and the University of Chicago Graduate School of Business. Our students are some of the brightest business minds in the country and have been active, if not willing, participants in helping to shape our thinking on the various topics.

While the people mentioned above inspired and challenged our thinking, the book would not have happened without the hard work of our book team. We give special thanks to Tom Kuczmarski, author of several books, and the man who encouraged the undertaking of this book project from the very beginning and shaped it along the way. Likewise, we give special thanks to Jonathan Sills for providing tremendous energy, research, structure to our thinking when it didn't exist, and tangible examples throughout the writing of the first draft. We give special thanks to Suzanne Lowe for editing and shaping our early drafts. She truly perservered and never lost faith in us despite setbacks and dry spells. Finally, we give special thanks to Burton Middlebrooks and Mary Neimer for the final edits that produced a reasonably clean manuscript for our publisher.

We were fortunate to have several people actively contribute to the research of the book. We give thanks to Kim Bradley, Tina Longoria, and Erika Seamon. We called upon several of our closest associates and sheepishly "allowed" them to review and edit specific chapters of our early writings. We give thanks to Diane Dahl, Scott Davis, Darrell Douglass, our editor Danielle Egan-Miller, Rich Hagel, and Randy Grudzinski. Finally, three individuals helped to keep all the pieces coming and going to the right people and, thus, we thank Deanna Justak, Eva Maleki, and Patty Sapien.

While the help from the people mentioned above regarding our thinking and written execution was invaluable, so too was the moral support and encouragement we received at a very personal level from several people. We give heartfelt thanks to additional encouragers— Joanne Bradley, Patty Middlebrooks, Rob Schultz, and Loreen Sieroslawski. These friends put the wind in our sails to start, gave us the courage to continue through the rough waters, splashed water on our faces when we wallowed in procrastination, and celebrated with us when we crossed the finish line.

To all, thank you for taking the journey with us!

PREFACE

*Taking a breath to steady his nerves, the CEO of RestEasy, a
nationwide hotel chain, stepped to the lectern to address the
company's annual meeting. After leading the company on an
extended effort to bolster revenues and profits, he was about to
deliver the bad news: market share was continuing to drop, and
competitors were continuing to attract an alarming percentage
of RestEasy's previously loyal customers. He reviewed the many
improvements that he had fostered: faster check-in and checkout times; standardized procedures for cleaning hotel rooms;
quality training for front desk clerks and concierges; the estab-
lishment of a frequent visitor program; and the addition of in-
room fax machines. He had to admit that his management
wizardry, so effective in the early days before strong competitors
emerged, had done nothing to slow RestEasy's slide into last
place behind the market leaders in the hotel industry.*

MANY OF TODAY'S SERVICE COMPANIES ARE
starting to recognize that they are at a similar defining moment as
this fictitious hotel chain: their strategies to mimic competitors
through better management and better quality ultimately leads to
competitive parity. And parity causes customers to make decisions on
the basis of price, which leads to lower profits. For example, throughout the early 1990s, the top three domestic airline companies lost
millions of dollars, while Southwest Airlines prospered. The "leading" companies reengineered, outsourced, reorganized, and tried just
about every other "be better" program. Yet these incremental, "copy

cat" solutions have not enabled them to look different from competitors nor to sustain any significant competitive edges to attract more profitable customers.

The burgeoning service sector stands today at the crossroads of its evolution where doing things better is no longer the formula for success. Executives and managers in service companies must begin to follow strategies that make customers see and feel unique value in their services. There needs to be a new battle cry within service organizations: Be a market leader!

Service companies are vastly different from product companies. Yet they often apply the marketing strategies and approaches designed for product companies. In particular, most leaders in today's service companies are trapped into thinking *better, faster, cheaper.* They engage in these cost-oriented activities to win the internal battle, only to find they are still losing the marketplace war. This is a costly and demoralizing trap. The managers in most service organizations haven't figured out that the key to Southwest Airlines's continued success is its abandonment of a product-centered, market-insensitive, operations-driven mind-set. Southwest's "do things differently" success is grounded on two principles: (1) to be, in fact, a *service* company, and (2) to be perceived as different from competitors by a targeted group of customers.

Why have some service companies grabbed and sustained market leadership in their industry? Over the past fifteen years, our experience in consulting with scores of service companies and conducting research across a broad range of service industries—including environmental services, financial services, health care, insurance, information database services, information technology services, Internet services, networking services, professional services, publishing, retail, telecommunications, transportation, travel, and electric and gas utilities—has led us to the conclusion that service market leaders rarely rise through serendipity. These market leaders:

- orient their entire organization toward delivering new, unique benefits
- focus their company's efforts and target profitable segments of customers

- understand that their service has a brand identity, and invest in it and treat it like a long-term asset
- deliver new benefits through a broad portfolio of service innovations
- reinvent their current services and create new services to meet the changing needs of their target customers and to address the inevitable commodification of their service offerings
- differentiate themselves by using their service delivery process to give a narrowly focused segment of customers a unique and beneficial experience
- put employees in the equation by enabling them to become fully engaged in the business of service to customers
- put processes in place to sustain market leadership over the long run
- recognize the need to reinvent their core business and services before the bottom falls out—and they do it

A select few, such as Southwest Airlines, Wal-Mart, Charles Schwab, and Taco Bell, have set their sights on doing business in a different way from their competitors. Their ways are inspiring, and their companies are thriving. In today's maturing service sector, the majority of service companies are *not* leading—they are following. And the "followers" will continue to fall behind the companies that make service leadership an everyday occurrence. The followers desperately need to understand the significance and power of the service marketing strategies that the leaders use.

Market Leadership Strategies for Service Companies argues emphatically that adopting a philosophy of "doing things differently" is more powerful than "doing things better." It shows that developing and implementing marketing strategies to be different—tailored specifically for service companies—is the only way to win in increasingly price-competitive and commodity-like service industries.

Market Leadership Strategies for Service Companies demonstrates how continuous innovation is critical to gaining and sustaining a leadership position. Services tend to be rapidly duplicated, and without a continuous-innovation mind-set, service companies fall prey to price wars and declining profits. An innovation mind-set, process, and focused resources are needed to deliver continuous waves of new value to the marketplace.

Market Leadership Strategies for Service Companies shows the importance of connecting all employees to the organization's superordinate goal of offering truly unique and value-added services. Overengineered employees desperately need to once again pursue the most personally satisfying service goal: doing things that make a difference in the eyes of customers. Company efforts to routinize and standardize have caused literally millions of service employees to feel robotic in their daily execution of quality, cycle-time reduction, reengineering, and a host of other operational activities that merely perpetuate the organization. This book shows how service companies can unleash the personalities of their people so customers can have beneficial, individually tailored service experiences that cannot be easily duplicated by competitors.

It is time for a change. *Market Leadership Strategies for Service Companies* reveals the copycat trap many service companies have fallen into and identifies the root causes of this trap. This book offers specific strategies for service companies to become market leaders and sustain a dominant position in fiercely price-competitive, commodity-like markets.

MARKET LEADERSHIP STRATEGIES

FOR SERVICE COMPANIES

PART I

Adopting a "Be Different" Attitude

CHAPTER 1

If You Are a Service Company... Then Be a Service Company

FOR THE PAST TWO DECADES, SERVICE INDUS-
tries and service companies have emerged from relative obscurity in
our business community. They now dominate the U.S. economy
accounting for nearly 70 percent of our GNP and more than 70 percent of our workforce in 1998.

Unfortunately, most service companies have not yet found the
recipe for achieving profitable growth in today's increasingly complex
and competitive environment. Under the banner of becoming more
marketing savvy and customer-focused, many managers are trying to
market and grow their *service* company as though it were a *product*
company. They become overly focused on the tangible elements—
e.g., product features, operational efficiency, and the like—and
neglect to develop strategies for differentiating, innovating, and marketing the intangible service experience. But the uniqueness and
value of the service experience is what the customers really care
about.

The mistake of "productizing" a service offering usually leads to
perceived parity with others, and customers resort to buying on the
basis of price and features. That is why thousands of people switch
long-distance carriers every month for a $50 check—they do not

perceive a meaningful difference between providers. Because many service companies focus almost exclusively on the "product characteristics," they are experiencing drastically shrinking profit margins.

Service companies are unique—marketing and managing an intangible experience is different. Service companies need to find ways to:

- define their service business and the benefits customers receive
- bring out the intangible aspects of the service experience
- lead their company into a different direction from competitors by addressing new, intense, unmet customer needs
- put people back into the equation, not just automate and reengineer to increase operational efficiency
- adopt market leadership strategies that get service companies out of the parity battles being fought today

Focusing on these imperatives will help service companies create experiences that bring customers back time and again. This chapter provides an overview of the key elements a service company should focus on to become a dominant market leader.

Defining Your Service Business and Customer Benefits

Differentiating your company from others can be done only if you know what business you are in and what benefits customers derive from your existence. And differentiation can be done only if a company remains clearly defined for a period of three to five years in relatively stable markets. As the old adage goes, "Know thyself—and to thine own self be true." Specifically, many service companies need to:

- proactively determine the desired mix of services and products in their offerings
- understand that their investments in costly assets and internal operations may *not* be what really attracts customers or keeps them coming back
- put service back into the equation

Misunderstanding the nature of one's service business often stems from not knowing what combination of service and product constitutes the offering. For example, are fast-food restaurants in the service or product business? It depends. Domino's is more of a service business, whereas Pizza Hut is more focused on product. McDonald's has been competing primarily as a food product company almost since its inception. Taco Bell recently changed strategies and moved from a product focus to more of a service orientation. It did so by removing much of the food preparation operation from restaurants and increasing the number of Taco Bell employees interacting with customers. Even with different approaches, all of these companies continue to be successful business enterprises.

Other sets of service industries caught up in misunderstanding the nature of their businesses are those that have huge and costly operations and infrastructures—such as airlines, hotels, telecommunication companies, equipment leasing companies, and railroads. Providers in these industries tend to get stuck right in the middle of the service-product continuum by acting as though they are in the "asset rental" business—i.e., a seat, room, time on the telephone network, equipment, or space on a train for rent.

Service companies stop differentiating themselves when their operations and physical assets become the end mission instead of a means to an end. This asset orientation requires enormous capital and, in competitive markets, receives a "ho-hum" response from customers. For example, consider railroad customers who are concerned with on-time delivery. One railroad may tout to its customers the hundreds of millions of dollars it has invested in new, faster, and more durable locomotives. Speed of the asset, however, will not necessarily win over the customers desiring on-time delivery. A competing railroad might focus instead on perfecting a system that allows customers at any time to change their requested delivery time to coincide with their plant's changing schedule and small inventory storage capacity. This "delivery on demand" service may still require significant investment in infrastructure. However, it propels the company into the service side of the business and innovates by delivering an experience customers are willing to either pay more or switch providers for.

Finally, industries that have been monopolistic or previously regulated by the government often misunderstand the nature of their service business. Gas and electric utilities and phone companies are prime examples. These companies are often run like product companies that deliver a commodity requiring no human interaction. In fact, customers only interact with the company when they receive a bill or if they have a problem. The service is not in the picture. Most customers are treated alike and assumed to have similar needs. The key to successful growth for these companies is to put service back into the equation and move toward the service end of the spectrum.

Consider the music industry and how different companies might define their business as either primarily a product or primarily a service business. Assume that "listening enjoyment" is the experience customers are buying. If company A sells prerecorded music on compact discs, it is a provider of products. If company B adds music teachers to its staff to educate customers on how best to listen to music, it has started to use services to create different strategic benefits for them. But if company C wants to redefine its core business to be a pure service business, what might that look like? Perhaps it would be a company that sells "usage time" instead of tangible CD products and, therefore, uses the CDs as enablers of the service. Through a toll-free number and direct mail, company C might rent its inventory of CDs on a weekly or monthly basis. Alternatively, it might create a service called "music on demand," in which a customer could access any music inventory through their on-line personal computer and play it through their digital sound system.

Shown in Figure 1.1 are some examples of competitors in the same industry that are strategically defined differently on the service-product continuum. Any position on the continuum can result in

Figure 1.1 **The Service-Product Continuum**

Services with enablers	Services with products	Asset Rental	Products with value-adding services	Products with supporting services
	Domino's		Pizza Hut	
Movies/Music on Demand				Videos and Compact Discs
		AT&T		Microsoft
	Investment Banking		Corporate Banking	
Southwest		United		

success. The point is to know what type of business you are in and what benefits customers expect from doing business with you.

Focusing on the Intangibles, Not Just the Tangibles

Confusion about whether a company offers more of a service or product usually also leads to an improper focus on tangibles. The trap for many service companies is not understanding the roles of the tangible and intangible elements of the services offered. The majority tend to err on the side of overemphasizing and promoting the tangibles while almost ignoring the intangibles.

For example, the technology consulting industry is known for focusing on the tangible methodologies that explain the process they go through to address a client's needs. The methodologies are often touted in lieu of the intangible expertise of the people who actually do the work. While methodologies are good for promoting quality, they are unhelpful and often damaging for companies pursuing differentiation. The reason is simple. A service is an experience that customers feel and remember. The other physical senses do not come into play as they do with products. And the people, not the methodology, deliver the service experience.

Developing and delivering intangibles that make the service unique is a critical challenge for service companies. In order to be different, the intangibles should be those relating to the actual experience or performance. Figure 1.2 (page 8) helps illustrate this thinking.

These examples include competitors from two similar industries. Each defines itself differently on the service-product continuum and each, consequently, has different distinguishing intangibles. If Pizza Hut pursued a rapid-delivery guarantee, it would be focusing on the wrong intangible—one that's already taken and is inconsistent with its core offering. While it has not yet done so, it would seem Pizza Hut could focus on the intangible of "customizing the taste" for home pizza eaters. This could entail innovations in packaging, unique "for home consumption only" ingredients, and new services. For example, Pizza Hut could develop recipes that allow customers to apply ingredients themselves to customize the pizza. It might also train and promote their delivery people as "home service waiters"—meaning they

Figure 1.2 **Competing on the Intangibles**

Core Offering	Memory	Intangible Actions	Expectations
Domino's: delivery service	Fast delivery	• 30-minute time frame • Selected food, hot at home • Pleasant drivers with change	• Guarantee of 30 minutes • Easy to order with one number
Pizza Hut: pizza product delivered	Great taste	• Great looking and tasting pizza at home • Pizza properly boxed and handled • Unique taste and ingredients	• Testimonials regarding taste • Free trials
Southwest: no-frills transport	Fun and cheap trip	• Performance of flight attendants • Pay for extras • Atmosphere of cabin-passenger involvement	• Price of ticket lower than others
Delta: full service airline	Professional transportation	• On-time arrival • Equipment handled in all elements/situations • All passenger personal needs handled	• High quality and safety • Preflight service setup (seat, meals)

cut and serve the pizza at the customers' homes. Now these would be really focusing on the intangibles!

Retail banks offer another example of the criticality of intangibles for service companies. The only tangibles customers can walk away with are cash and some sort of statement or report. But these tangibles do not define why customers select or remain with a particular bank. Rather, customers encounter a wide range of experiences that are mostly intangible. These experiences may include getting cash at any time from a convenient location, having a safe storage place for money, accessing knowledgeable experts about how to invest, moving money between investments whenever customers want, and so on. Unfortunately, the innovation efforts of banks rarely address these intangible and experiential elements. Instead, banks spend millions on sophisticated computer systems, comprehensive (and confusing) reporting, new technologies for operational efficiencies, and the like—all under some sort of innovation banner. But they have forgotten about the intangible experiences of customers. Since the automated teller machines (ATMs) of the late 1970s and accounts that give access to many banking and nonbanking products of the early 1980s, what innovations have occurred in retail banking relative to the *customers'* experiences? If banks had not been forced to embrace the Internet, there would be no answer. The intense and expensive efforts on the tangible features have not dramatically created new and loyal customers, which is the goal of market leaders.

Leading the Way to "Be Different"

Service company leaders regularly face defining moments. They must keep their team focused on being a service company while challenging them to do things differently in the marketplace, things that will truly affect their leadership position. Can you identify with the following story?

> *The ship was sailing in fourth place in the year's biggest regatta. Suddenly, the crew began shouting in desperation to their captain, "What is your decision? Should we go north of the island like the lead ships in the race, or should we go through the uncharted waters south of the island?" The captain suddenly realized he was facing a defining moment. North meant going toe-to-toe with the other ships in order to win. It meant focusing efforts on operating the ship better than rivals who would be using the same sailing techniques to navigate the well-known challenges of the northern course. "If we could just execute better and more efficiently than the others, we might be able to come in third, maybe even second," the captain thought.*
>
> *Going south through uncharted waters, on the contrary, meant focusing efforts on navigating the ship differently than competitors in order to win. This choice had significant risks but, being a shorter route, also increased their odds of actually*

winning the race. Winning would be a matter of the captain and crew's level of adaptability against the challenges of the lesser-known environment.

The captain rightfully knew this was a defining moment for his team. Should they do things better than competitors or do things differently? With excitement and decisiveness he roared, "Let's be different and win this race! Southward!"

Today's maturing and stagnant service industries desperately need to understand the significance and power of the strategies these mariners discovered. Adopting an overall philosophy of "doing things differently" is more powerful in the marketplace than "doing things better." Developing and implementing new strategies to be different is the only way to win in increasingly price-competitive and commodity-like industries. An overemphasis on quality, efficiency, and standardization is, in fact, a major cause of a service company's inability to differentiate itself from competitors or to energize its people to provide extraordinary service.

At most service companies, the movement of reengineering has gone too far. Reengineering produces a focus on internal efficiency and blurs the importance of external effectiveness in beating the competition. Companies have become smaller and faster but not smarter. As a result, they have fallen victim to an internal myopia of cost reduction at the expense of building a defensible competitive position in the marketplace for future profitable growth. Companies need to implement a process that uncovers opportunities, aligns strategies, and allocates resources in order to invent real growth.

Quality programs are another example of where service companies have focused too much effort at the expense of dominant market leadership. Too much quality is bad when it comes at the expense of innovation. Many service companies today have a mind-set of benchmarking the competition so as to be like everyone else, instead of innovating to be unique. These companies are having a hard time demonstrating to customers that their quality is far superior to that of competitors. They have, in effect, created among their customers a "who cares" attitude regarding quality, while they continue to exert herculean efforts and spend millions to improve quality. While most companies are trapped trying to do things better with their existing business, the true competitive advantage lies in redefining the business and the benefits provided to customers.

Putting People Back into the Equation

Overengineered employees desperately need to once again pursue the most personally satisfying work goal: doing things that make a difference in the eyes of customers. Employees intuitively know that their core mission should be to provide the kind of help to customers that is truly needed and that no one else could provide. Their company's seeming indifference to being perceived by customers as unique has frustrated them. This indifference to the needs of the marketplace is further exacerbated by senior management's obsession to "right-size" and standardize every few years. The net effect is that millions of employees feel robotic in their daily execution of quality, cycle-time reduction, reengineering, and a host of other "operational" activities that merely perpetuate rather than improve the company. These people must be marshaled cohesively to implement a set of understandable and inspiring strategies.

Employees are often the most misunderstood, underutilized, and overstructured asset of service companies. But next to customers, they are the second most valuable assets that companies have. The problem lies in the perception of the role that employees play in the customer experience. Many service companies view their employees simply as part of a process that produces an end output—a physical product to be delivered to a customer. If a customer's primary focus is on the functional performance of that physical product, the employees generally do not need to be involved with the customer's experience. But with services the situation should be different. In fact, in most service companies the employees are very involved in the customer's experience. The mistake made by well-meaning and well-schooled service managers is to dehumanize their people—all in the name of quality control. Service managers attempt to make employees virtually interchangeable. Although industrializing the service process may be important and even necessary, taking the "perform-ers" out of the equation leads to a neutered, indistinguishable experi-ence for customers.

Schlesinger and Heskett of the Harvard Business School have es-tablished a new model for service employees. It is based on the precept that the employee-as-disposable-tool model, which leads to job over-simplification and idiot proofing, is very costly to a service company. Their model includes four key elements:

1. valuing investments in people just as much as investments in technology
2. using technology to support, not to replace, frontline people
3. putting as much emphasis on selection and training for front-line employees (e.g., salesclerks and housekeepers) as for man-agers and executives
4. linking compensation and performance for employees at every level

Managers who are not currently implementing this new model are trapped into believing productivity and quality improvement gains will come from "tightening up the ship" and, in particular, tossing some shipmates overboard. But quality is a moving target based on each customer's gauge of the unique experience they received as com-pared to the expectations they intuitively established. Productivity and quality improvement come from having people involved with customers—people who want the responsibility, can manage them-selves, respond well to pressure from customers, and who are highly motivated through skills, job opportunities, and pay advancements. We will have more to say about employees in Chapters 11 and 12.

Adopting Market Leadership Strategies to Overcome Parity Battles

Every service company is a potential victim of the parity battle. The majority of service companies today are embroiled in bitter and unprofitable day-to-day battles for leadership within their highly competitive industries. Their industries are mired in a state of parity in which customers differentiate on price and availability. Can you pick out the industries from the following list that are experiencing intense parity battles today?

Health care	Information services consulting
Insurance	Oil and gas
Banking	Chemicals
Accounting	Railroad
Brokerage	Trucking
Fast food	Ocean shipping
Telecommunications	Overnight mail
Airline	Waste hauling
Gas and electric utilities	Public education
General retail	Tax preparation

You are right if you picked all of them. The reality is that all these industries, and many others, face severe customer indifference. What companies in these industries need is a new, company-wide focus on market leadership strategies.

Mini Maids is an example of a service company that pioneered a new industry, establishing the quality standards that customers came to expect, only to watch competitors duplicate and drag the whole industry into its present commodity state. It is a classic example of too much focus on quality at the expense of innovation and, ultimately, at the expense of growth and profitability. And it is by no means an isolated case; this situation, unfortunately, exists in many of today's service industries and markets.

Mini Maids was the maid service pioneer in a billion-dollar cleaning-service industry that barely existed twenty years ago. The company was built on the concepts of teamwork, efficiency, and standardization. Every franchisee receives a 300-page operations manual following McDonald's approach to service quality control. Further, Mini Maids brings their own equipment and cleaning supplies in order to guarantee a standard job. They furnish a list of exactly what services they will provide, and a follow-up phone call the next day is customary practice to check for customer satisfaction. These efforts and many others are great for continuous quality improvements, but they no longer differentiate the service nor deliver new, valued benefits for customers. Simply put, Mini Maids has failed to continue to strategically approach the market and innovate. And, sadly, it remains a very small player in the industry it helped create.

Today, Mini Maids has many competitors including Mega Maids, Custom Maids, McMaids, and just about every other cleaning outfit one could imagine. Most maid services promote their "greater quality" through guarantees and testimonials, but the major players have all reached sufficient quality levels in the eyes of customers—so quality is no longer a factor in selection. Some maid services focus on business customers while others concentrate on residential cleaning. But where is the hard-core differentiation? There is none. The prime offering has become a commodity—maid services—and the service process is still the same: someone, usually low skilled, coming regularly to your home or office to clean.

The application of market leadership strategies serves to increase the perceived benefits to customers. But more important, it focuses on externally innovating the service rather than on enhancing internal operations. A new maid-service concept is presented in Figure 1.3 (page 15), which defines new strategies to impact customers.

It starts with examining customers' homes, routines, and lives, and uncovering areas of intense need. In so doing, suppose there was a sizable segment of customers who want their house organized as well as cleaned. Defining the new service business as house management incorporates several additional new, valued benefits, such as organizing the house in addition to cleaning it. This business could eventually be expanded to address other noncleaning related house management needs—for example, routine home maintenance and minor repairs.

Second, the unique customer benefit needs to be communicated in a way that's different from competitors. The benefit "Your House Will Be Clean and Organized" would establish a whole new niche within the category of home-cleaning service. Dividing an industry into niche segments can be almost endless and has the power of allowing you to be first in a particular niche (see Chapters 4, 5, and 6). For example, in Europe a new residential cleaning segment was created and communicated as "your house will be clean and you'll be entertained." One particular cleaning-service company delivered on this promise by having the maids perform the cleaning in the nude—talk about differentiation!

Figure 1.3 **Strategic Innovation of Maid Services**

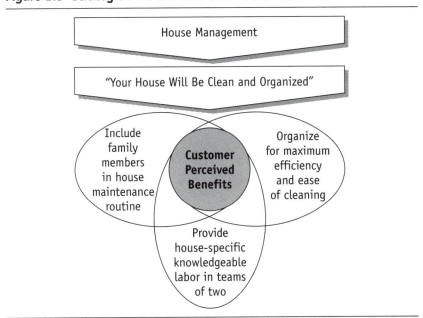

Third, other new market leadership strategies include innovating the service concepts, service process, and people delivery components:

- The service concept could be innovated to include products and services that help a home owner stay organized (e.g., filing systems, storage systems, closet systems, etc.).
- The service process or experience could be innovated to include family members as part of the house maintenance routine.
- The people delivery system could be innovated by having employees return each week to the same homes so they obtain knowledge and expertise about each home.

Conclusion

When service companies focus too much on the "product" characteristics—the tangible elements of their service—they typically experience shrinking profit margins. Successful service market leaders never forget the fundamental truth that they are marketing and managing

Figure 1.4 **The Seven Strategies for Service Market Leadership**

Chapters 1–3

1. Service Business Definition
- Determine position on the service-product continuum
- Establish a "be different" attitude

Chapters 4–5

2. Target Market Innovation
- Uncover unmet needs and underserved segments
- Select areas of focus

Chapter 6

3. Brand Positioning Innovation
- Establish a brand identity
- Decide how you will be different

Chapters 7–9

4. Service Offering Innovation
- Uncover customer problems
- Rapidly develop/launch market-driven solutions

Chapter 10

5. Process Experience Innovation
- Create a customer-valued process
- Design for judgment

Chapter 11

6. People Innovation
- Define new and unique roles
- Train for/allow individualized service experiences

Chapters 12–14

7. Sustaining Leadership
- Develop the supporting processes and marketing mind-set
- Redefine the franchise for the future

an intangible experience. They focus on the intangible aspects that create the service. The starting point is to understand whether the organization offers a pure service or a service-product, then determine and emphasize the intangible actions that create a valuable experience for customers.

Service market leaders demonstrate that adopting a philosophy of doing things differently is more powerful in the marketplace than doing things better. This is especially true today since most service markets are increasingly price sensitive and commodity-like. In pursuing a "be different" goal, many service companies misunderstand the role of front line employees. These employees want to pursue the most personally satisfying work goal: doing things that make a difference in the eyes of customers. In most service companies, front line employees are very involved in the customer's experience. A commonly made mistake is to view them as virtually interchangeable and to make the service process too routinized. The answer is to put the people "performers" back in the service experience equation for customers.

This first three chapters of this book discuss *why* service companies need to dare to be different and execute the recommended market leadership strategies. The remaining chapters then provide the specific strategies for *how* a service company can prosper by being different from competitors. Figure 1.4 outlines the seven strategies for service market leadership.

These seven strategies provide an approach for narrowing the growth opportunities in the marketplace in order to provide focus for inventing new customer benefits and increasing customer value—the essential ingredients for being different. Applying these strategies leads to inventing growth and becoming a market leader. The dark days of stagnation due to downsizing and re-engineering are over. The era of corporate invention and innovation is here. Finding *your* customers and creating what they will want *tomorrow*, before competitors do, is now the imperative.

CHAPTER 2

Avoid the "Be Better" Trap

SERVICE COMPANIES HAVE BECOME SEVERELY addicted to overmanaging the internal operations, processes, and people. Leaders and managers too often worry about comparisons of their company to competitors or to the "stretch" goals of continuous improvement. This is similar to improving a home to keep up with the Joneses or with the neighbors just to make something work a little better than it does now. In managing a service business, comparisons become unhealthy when there are no balancing strategies for producing a competitive edge with customers.

Several years ago, the comparison addiction of one of the largest U.S. banks had reached such a severe level that revenue growth was paralyzed. Over a five-year period, the bank developed and implemented a rigorous quality, continuous improvement, and benchmarking program and established more than five hundred quantifiable measures to determine how well the program was being implemented. These measures often were analyzed and reported on a daily or weekly basis! The organization became embroiled in a hotbed of memo-writing and meetings to continuously fix the "manage the business better" issues that surfaced in these reports. Unfortunately, these management improvement activities did not produce a competitive edge with customers.

The "Be Better" Trap Is Pervasive

The "be better" trap is one into which service companies can easily fall—getting out is considerably more difficult. Most companies simply do not see the symptoms along the way. They build up a false sense of security and a cultural blindness to the health of their business in the marketplace. They pursue "be better" activities with the intention of creating a dramatic market impact. All too often, however, they pursue myths that don't result in market leadership. Some of the myths are illustrated in Figure 2.1.

Usually, it is much easier to witness from a customer's perspective a company or industry caught in parity than it is from an internal evaluation. Ask yourself this question: "Which of the following airlines—United, Delta, or American—have created new, meaningful, and unique value for me?" This is a tough question for you and I—the customers—to answer. It is an even tougher question for airline managers to answer and then deliver upon. Have you ever flown on Southwest Airlines? What new, meaningful, and unique value does this airline provide? This is a much easier question to answer. Southwest Airlines provides an entertaining and more intimate flying experience. The

Figure 2.1 **Myths of "Be Better" Approaches**

"Be Better" Approach		Market Impact Myth
Pursuit of high quality	⟶	Win and keep customers by reducing errors
Standardized operations	⟶	Win customers on reliability
"Be big" for scale economies	⟶	Win customers as low-cost provider
Reengineering	⟶	Keep customers with more responsive processes
Integrated information systems	⟶	Keep customers through technology barriers
Benchmarking	⟶	Win customers with best-of-breed operations

flight attendants engage with customers, such as by using clever poems or jingles to give the mandatory safety pitch before the flight takes off. Further, their "sit where you want" approach to boarding the plane creates a more family-like atmosphere among passengers. These differentiators also come with the benefit of a low price for a flight—which is always appreciated. And the fact is Southwest Airlines was the only profitable U.S. airline during the first half of the 1990s. They did it by creating unique value.

Another example of parity can be found in the fast-food industry, which is populated with fierce competitors. There are hamburger places, chicken places, Mexican food places, chicken and hamburger places, chicken-hamburger-Mexican food places, sit-down restaurants, drive-thrus, sit-down and drive-thrus, eat-ins, delivery onlys, eat-ins and deliveries, and about a hundred other variations. This industry is also filled with many well-established brands, including McDonald's, Burger King, Wendy's, Kentucky Fried Chicken, Popeye's Chicken, Domino's Pizza, Pizza Hut, and the like. Again, ask yourself "Which fast-food companies have created new, meaningful, and unique value for me?" Aside from the unique food type, this is a tough question to answer. They all offer speed, acceptable food quality, menu choices, and consistency in service and convenience. The trap of parity is certainly difficult for managers in this industry. However, during the last several years, Wendy's, Taco Bell, and Subway have all achieved revenue growth and gross margins at the top of the industry. Do you think any of the three were trying to answer the question of new, meaningful, and unique value? Obviously, many customers did.

How about automobile insurance companies? There are many to choose from, such as State Farm, Allstate, and Farmers. Again, "Which of these have created new, meaningful, and unique value for me?" Aside from those of us who may have a highly skilled agent, most customers' selections are based on price because the service seems about the same to them. Enter Progressive Insurance. Through most of the 1990s, Progressive was the fastest growing and had the highest gross margins among all the large automobile insurance companies. They have built a service reputation by providing fast application approval and fast in-person response and resolution when a customer has an accident or problem. While their approach may seem fundamental to running a service-oriented insurance business, from a customer's perspective, Progressive created new, meaningful, and unique value.

What about the service and maintenance organizations of heavy equipment manufacturers? Or the residential real estate industry? Or upscale hotel chains? Or discount brokerage companies? If you are like most customers, only a few company names come to mind when asking who provides the customer with new, meaningful, and unique value. What a tragedy for all the other companies caught in the "be better" trap.

Strategies to make a company be like every other competitor is marketplace suicide. Being in a parity situation inevitably leads to a declining customer base and lower profits.

Types of "Be Better" Traps

Two approaches tend to trap service companies and prevent them from becoming enduring market leaders:

1. The continuous improvement trap occurs when a service company offers new programs, features, or operational improvements that deliver little or no new value to customers.
2. The comparison trap occurs when service companies compare against and strive to one-up current competitors.

The Continuous Improvement Trap—an Inward Focus

One of the primary myths believed by service companies is that becoming better and more efficient in running operations will guarantee success in the marketplace. Management falls into a trap—they convince themselves that all their efforts and investments to improve internal operations and be slightly better than competitors will also produce new value for customers. In reality, customers often respond through their purchasing habits with a bored "Who cares?" Try this on yourself. What ran through your mind when you last received mail from a hotel offering a promotion where you could accumulate points toward a free night's stay? Did you:

a. Rush to the phone to schedule a year's worth of hotel stays?
b. Draft a memo asking your travel agent to only book you at this hotel?
c. Complete the form and send it back since you stay at that hotel anyway?
d. Throw the letter in the garbage?

Potential customers would probably perceive this new program as similar to everyone else's. But the hotel company spent good money developing new features to make it more attractive than its competitors' programs. They built state-of-the-art information systems, developed new customer service capabilities, and created new ways to tell potential customers about the program. But all to no avail. Nothing really differentiates this company in the customers' mind from its competitors with like programs.

In similar fashion, the retail bank mentioned earlier was trapped in a "be better" approach that was disconnected from customer needs. One year, their customer service operation answered phone calls, on average, within five rings. The next year, they established a goal of four rings. And the next year, three rings. And the next year, two rings. Millions of dollars were invested to improve systems, hire and train staff, and educate employees on the new processes. Unfortunately, the improvements were never tested with customers. The net result: phones were indeed answered in two rings, but customers continued to leave the bank. Why? Because customers did not value this rather insignificant improvement and many others like it. The bank was not substantially unique when compared to others.

Ultimately, customers determine what programs, improvements, and services they value.

The Comparison Trap—a Competitor Copycat Focus

The most damaging feature of service companies caught in a "be better" trap surfaces when their business improvement strategies are built upon a heritage of comparison programs. These initiatives often accelerate the loss of competitive edge with customers. In the absence of true strategies that uniquely fulfill customers' needs, management can overextend operational improvement strategies focused on competitor benchmarking, quality improvement, low-cost operations, and the like.

The downward spiral accelerates when several leading companies in the industry are also addicted to comparison programs and "be better" management strategies. Many "good" competitors end up striving to be a little better than the others, with all offering similar value to customers. The trap is a profit-killing tit-for-tat exercise where competitors do not pursue significant differentiation and customers don't perceive any. When customers see no difference among service providers, they see relative parity; and parity causes customers to select on the basis of price, which inevitably leads to lower profits. This trap can be the death knell of a business.

Many of today's service companies are at a crossroads. They have followed strategies and tactics to continuously improve or be better than they were in prior years. The managers must now decide whether or not to pursue strategies that dramatically differentiate themselves from competitors in the eyes of their customers and prospects.

Causes of the "Be Better" Trap

Having examined scores of service companies, we have identified four *internal* causes and four *marketplace* causes of the "be better" trap. The four *internal* causes relate to:

1. cost-side fixation
2. too much standardization
3. "be like the leader" obsession
4. "get something out the door" syndrome

While these elements may indeed be noble and are, in fact, often needed in small doses, their overindulgence by companies usually leads to trouble.

Not all service companies that fall into the "be better" trap do so by their own hand or strategies. Many simply compete in an environment that is already in a "commodified" state. Customers perceive that all providers offer commodity-like services and products. Four marketplace symptoms lead companies into the "be better" trap:

1. reduction in the "wow factor"
2. market diversity and fragmentation
3. reactions to loud customers
4. reduced impact of new introductions

Internal Causes of the "Be Better" Trap

Cost-Side Fixation

The problem for many service companies is that they think operations first, second, and third. Why? Because operations is a "this year," "now" occurrence. Most service organizations are squeezing every last dollar out of the cost-side of the equation, but are doing very little to improve revenue or gross profit margins. Major internal initiatives—such as implementing quality programs to achieve the Malcolm Baldrige award or developing state-of-the-art information systems—keep managers focused on the nuts and bolts of running the business. What happens? Everyone's eyes are taken off the prize—the customers.

Contrast that with a growth focus addressing the future—a focus concerned with market leadership, competitive differentiation, category expansion, niche exclusivity, value-embedded products and services, higher prices, increased sales per customer, customer partnerships, and brand equity.

The primary objective of most business enterprises is to make money for the owners. The only way to accomplish this is to win and keep profit-producing customers. They are the sole source of revenue for the business enterprise. As Theodore Levitt remarked in his book *Marketing Imagination*, "Without customers, no amount of engineering wizardry, clever financing or operations expertise can keep the company going." This simple but profound truism has been forgotten in most service organizations today.

And Peter Drucker remarks in his book *The Practice of Management*, "Marketing and innovation produce results; all the rest [of a business's activities] are costs." Cost-side activities, such as reengineering, strip from the organization's culture the will to invent new value for customers. Companies are trapped into trying to do things better within their area of business, forgetting, or never even realizing, that the true competitive advantage lies in innovating their area of the business itself—creating new, meaningful, and unique value for the customer.

Too Much Standardization

Too much standardization makes it too easy for customers to do comparison-shopping. In the late 1980s and early 1990s, FedEx was keenly focused on quality. Everything became standardized. In fact, delivery drivers' jobs became so routinized that even turning off the ignition was to be checked off a list of "to dos." As this standardization was accomplished across the organization, operational efficiency and effectiveness did indeed improve. So much so, in fact, that reporters and other company representatives wanting to know how they did it besieged FedEx's Memphis headquarters.

Then a strange thing happened. Competitors also became focused on quality and standardizing their operations. As such, standardization and high quality became the norm for the industry. And so did customers' perceptions of interchangeability among overnight delivery providers. Soon customers could not tell the difference and began switching providers on the basis of price.

"Be Like the Leader" Obsession

The leader wanna-bes in many industries are caught in a cruel game. Management drills into the troops the need to find out what the competitor is doing and to do it better. The scope and strategies of the business then become both defined and confined within the wake of the industry leader. It is a dismal corporate life—always playing catch-up and never really having a distinct identity.

Service companies caught in this trap also overemphasize the goal of *market share*, a term that too often ends up meaning "fair share" to the company culture. This, then, translates into an entitlement mind-set that reads "if we are 'as good as' the other leading companies, we will get our fair share of customers." But that is not so.

"Get Something Out the Door" Syndrome

There are indeed many companies that emphasize the value-creating side of their organization. Their problem often lies in the type of new products and services, the scope of marketing programs, or the type of company-wide integration strategy through which new things are being created and brought to market. Directives such as "Let's get new products out the door this year" result in a focus on the low-risk, incremental improvements. This gives the appearance that new products or services are a vital part of growing the business, but in actuality the company is trapped in another "slightly better" improvement initiative.

Similar results come from narrowly defined marketing programs driven by short-term needs and specific requests for tangible outputs such as brochures, advertising tag lines, and sales materials. Companies become trapped with marketing programs that only deliver messages to customers that say "we're good too," because these programs do not draw upon a long-term view or the full scope of activities of the company.

Marketplace Causes of the "Be Better" Trap

Reduction in the "Wow Factor"
Customers often stop being impressed by the capabilities and actions of even their best provider. The wow-factor wears off for a variety of reasons, creating a perspective of the provider as not being as valuable as before. For example, by the mid 1990s, customers were no longer impressed with having things shipped overnight and delivered to practically any location the next day (which even today is still an amazing feat). This caused severe price competition and profit pressure on FedEx, Airborne, UPS, and the other overnight carriers.

This evolution of falling perceptions of expertise is similar to the way most airline passengers feel about flying. Their fear of crashing is so far removed from their mind-set that the expertise of the pilots, mechanics, and the whole airline is no longer a consideration. Simply stated, their fear factor has been reduced dramatically. As a result, the entire industry has become so safe in the eyes of its customers that safety expertise has no perceived value. Providers who do not increase their expertise and brand equity in the eyes of their customers—or who continue to align their company's activities with a diminishing perceived need of customers (i.e., safe flying)—fall into the trap of doing all kinds of things, often at significant costs, that don't really matter to customers.

Market Diversity and Fragmentation
Most new markets start out with homogeneity—of customer needs, expectations, offerings, and the like. But similar to the evolution and diversity of offspring from Adam and Eve, markets are perpetually

moving away from their homogeneous past. They are seldom consolidating but, instead, are always dividing into ever-smaller groups of customers with similar needs. Companies that continue with programs and products for yesterday's consolidated segment of customers, rather than today's divided segments, fall into the trap of being perceived as offering a minimal level of value.

The small, homogeneous group of travelers who used to stay in the segment called "upscale hotels" doesn't really exist anymore. This group has divided into upscale customers who want all-suite rooms, upscale family travelers who want recreational accommodations, upscale pleasure travelers who want exclusivity in location and design—you name it. To be simply a provider of "upscale hotels" has little appeal to anyone in this now diverse market segment.

Reactions to Loud Customers
Have you ever been shouted at by a customer? Human nature tells people to avoid this situation. But when a service company gets into a pattern of only responding to the loudest customers, it will rapidly move toward the "be better" trap. This pattern breeds an insecure culture filled with the attitude of "let's just try to do a little better." Loud customers are angry about something done to or not done for them in the past. Even when placated, a provider usually only matches original expectations the customer had of all providers (otherwise they wouldn't have been shouting).

Of course every successful business must reduce the number of times their services or product performance fall short of expectations, and implement processes to make amends with customers when it does. However, a company that places most of its emphasis on fixing the problems of the past inevitably will be perceived by customers as trailing other competitors.

Reduced Impact of New Introductions
Competitive markets and sophisticated customers are very demanding of new product and service introductions. Essentially, customers expect the newest frill will provide greater value and be more unique than what already exists. From a provider's viewpoint, customers seem to award their purchasing dollars on the basis of this perspective.

For example, credit card holders were swayed in the past by "gold" levels of service, exclusive items to purchase through the mail, and the ability to accumulate points toward airline mileage awards. Providers became embroiled in a "feature frenzy" in which each tried to introduce a slightly new twist (read "frill") to the overall offering. While "be better" was rampant in the industry, no credit card provider had an impact with new product introductions since customers were no longer changing their purchasing behavior based on these features.

Are You Falling into the Trap?

Enough about everyone else. What about your company or business unit? Can you answer the value question posed earlier? If not, do you feel the "be better" trap coming? You will—it is just a matter of time.

Take the quiz in Figure 2.2. If you can answer "Agree" to more than one of the questions, it may mean that your organization needs to undergo a full "be better" cleansing, or at least begin balancing "be better" activities with strategies to be different.

Look back at your answers. If the majority of your check marks fall on the left side of the continuum, your organization truly needs to break free from the "be better" trap.

Figure 2.2 **"Be Better" Quiz**

	Relative to My Organization				
	Agree				Disagree
1. Lately, customers seem to select only according to price.	❏	❏	❏	❏	❏
2. Customers no longer value our sales force.	❏	❏	❏	❏	❏
3. Our new services and products are copied within months.	❏	❏	❏	❏	❏
4. Customers don't attach any benefits to our company's brand.	❏	❏	❏	❏	❏
5. Marketing and innovation play second fiddle to operations.	❏	❏	❏	❏	❏
6. Our sales people can't articulate what distinguishes us from competitors.	❏	❏	❏	❏	❏

Conclusion

Whether by their own internal breeding or by the market place environment, companies caught in the "be-better" trap struggle to achieve profitable growth. The following are common themes that managers from trapped companies talk about when attempting to get out of their predicament:

- prioritizing and selecting the appropriate growth opportunities—after new markets, new services, and new business opportunities have surfaced
- understanding the needs and problems of target customers and then creating new, value-adding solutions as a strategic and central element to running the business
- creating a unique identity in the marketplace that propels target customers to exclusively desire its products and services
- providing funding and management commitment to innovation, strategic marketing, growth planning, new service and product development, alliance partnerships, and brand equity
- changing the typical sales-and-operations-oriented culture and "beat the competition" mind-set to embrace the power of internally developed innovation to drive profitable business growth

What are the common elements of these themes? The need to:

1. instill the organizational disciplines that result in being perceived differently in the eyes of customers
2. marshal the resources to invent real growth

What's needed is a process for tying together the growth, marketing, and innovation elements of a business with its future growth opportunities and strategies. It must also become a strategic process that is part of the businesses' primary functions. Otherwise, the natural inclination toward cost-side management and unfocused, internal restructurings will quickly take hold again. Therefore, this book's purpose is to help readers get to the basics of implementing a "be different"—not a "be better"—approach.

CHAPTER 3

Dare to Be Different from Competitors

SERVICE COMPANIES NEED TO DARE TO BE different. To find a leadership position in the market . . . and then to *lead*. The key strategy is to be different from competitors. Service market leaders dominate their market niches by playing their own game, as opposed to one-upping competitors with the exact same offering. They break free from "be better," internally oriented initiatives to pursue "be-different," externally oriented strategies. Being different is grounded in providing customers with the unique value that they cannot get from any other competitor. It means constantly moving into uncharted waters and rallying the organization to do so confidently.

But why try to be different in the market? What end results are hoped for? The tangible results are accelerated growth. The intangible results are increased employee innovation and customer loyalty. And it's the intangible results that, for a service company, provide the foundation for long-term market leadership. McKinsey & Co. continues to dominate the highly competitive management consulting industry. They do so not only because they consistently produce a successful service, but also because they have built an incredible worldwide network of motivated, innovative, and interconnected people including employees, clients, academics, and former employees. They have created a different business approach that is unparalleled in the industry.

This chapter introduces the desired results from "be different" strategies—accelerated growth—as well as sources of growth. It also highlights the need for alternative "be different" approaches based on the stage of market life cycle, and the need to create a truly "be different" customer experience.

Pursuing Accelerated Growth

Service companies pursue strategies to be different from competitors and to be perceived that way in the minds of customers for a very simple reason: to achieve accelerated growth. But exactly what is accelerated growth? How is it different from other growth efforts and where does it fit within a company's overall framework and goals for growth? An accelerated growth goal for a company can be defined as a doubling of its traditional growth rate (*traditional* meaning either a company's historic or its industry's rate of growth). Thus, if a company has traditionally been growing at 10 percent per year, an accelerated growth goal would be to grow at 20 percent per year over the next five years.

To accomplish accelerated growth, a company must first continue to successfully manage and expand its revenues with current products and services to existing customers. But it must also pursue targeted new (and different) growth opportunities. These include new products and services, new ventures, new buyers within existing accounts, new niche markets, and new, noncore markets. For example, when McDonald's adds new items to its lunchtime menu, it is pursuing an initiative that helps it to accomplish traditional growth rates. But, when McDonald's more aggressively pursues market niches, such as kids, with new indoor play equipment that adds playtime to a kid's McDonald's experience, it is moving closer to achieving accelerated growth rates. "Be different" strategies provide the road map for companies wishing to achieve accelerated growth.

A helpful tool for communicating the size and appropriateness of an accelerated growth goal is a growth gap chart. This chart (Figure 3.1, page 33) summarizes the growth expectations of the current

Figure 3.1 **Growth Gap**

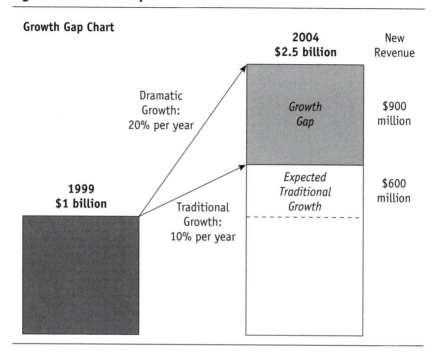

Growth Gap Chart

business and shows what additional new growth will need to be created in order to achieve the desired accelerated growth goal.

Sources of Accelerated Growth—the Growth Map

After determining the magnitude of desired growth, a second framework or tool can be used to show *where* the growth will come from and what type of investment will be needed. This framework is aptly called a growth map, because it helps companies match their market opportunities with efforts to create new value for customers.

As shown in Figure 3.2 on page 34, the three elements of the growth map are:

1. types of new products and services
2. types of new markets
3. types of growth investments

Figure 3.2 **Growth Map**

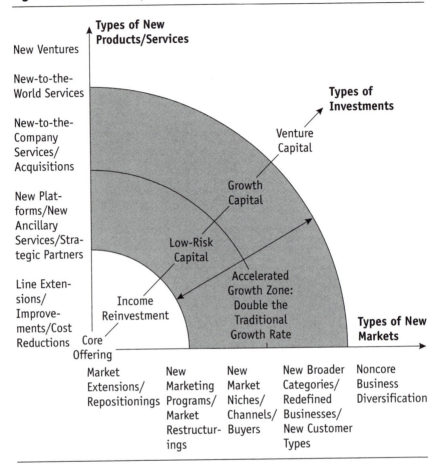

Types of New Products and Services

Companies need to establish goals and strategies for the types of new products and services they intend to launch. While there are usually opportunities for each type, companies traditionally pursue lower-risk choices. More will be said about this in Chapter 7. To achieve accelerated growth, goals must be set that include efforts in the shaded region on the growth map in Figure 3.2.

Figure 3.3 (page 35) shows how, in general, companies approach creating or generating different types of new products and services.

Figure 3.3 **New Service Approaches**

Type of New Product/ Service Desired		Activity for Implementing
New ventures	$\longrightarrow$	Start up new business unit
New-to-the-world services	$\longrightarrow$	Invent internally
New-to-the-company services/ acquisitions	$\longrightarrow$	Make or buy
New platforms/New ancillary services/Strategic partners	$\longrightarrow$	Make or lease or buy components
Line extensions/Improvements/ Cost reductions	$\longrightarrow$	Make only

Types of New Markets

Companies also need to establish goals and strategies for the types of future markets they intend to pursue. Once again, while the tendency is to focus on the markets of today, new types must be pursued to achieve accelerated growth. Figure 3.4 shows how, in general, companies approach the different types of new markets.

Figure 3.4 **New Market Approaches**

Type of New Market Desired		Activity for Implementing
Noncore business diversification	$\longrightarrow$	New markets and industries to address unrelated needs
New broader categories/Redefined businesses/New customer types	$\longrightarrow$	New strategic benefits to draw out unknown needs
New market niches/Channels/ Buyers	$\longrightarrow$	New targets and buyers to address new needs
New marketing programs/Market restructurings	$\longrightarrow$	New program designs to address unmet needs
Market extensions/Repositionings	$\longrightarrow$	Redesign to address unsatisfied needs

Types of Growth Investments

Investors (both internal and external) should think about the growth map as a way to calibrate their risk and return expectations. Internal growth champions often find it difficult to make the case for riskier investments such as developing new-to-the world services and entering into new categories. Incremental investments, such as cost reductions and line extensions, usually move through the system more easily. In order to achieve accelerated growth, companies need to become comfortable making riskier investments and thinking about a balanced portfolio of investments. Otherwise, they might as well give up now.

In addition to being a planning tool, the growth map can be used to indicate if a business is trapped in a commodity state and how rapidly the life cycle of the market is maturing. This is accomplished by plotting the company's current situation on the map at least once every year. To illustrate, Figure 3.5 shows FedEx's situation in the early 1990s, while Figure 3.6 (page 37) shows FedEx's situation in the later part of

Figure 3.5 **FedEx Growth Map—Early 1990s**

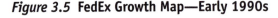

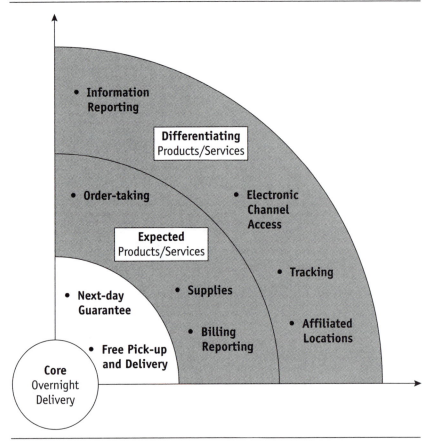

the 1990s. Notice how new offerings that were considered differentiating in the early 1990s have migrated to become expected services.

You will notice that the semicircular areas on the map take on new meanings. The first wave on the map represents the core market and service offering. This area requires significant operations, investments, and "be better" management programs in order to maintain its viability.

The second wave contains those ancillary or supplemental products and services that customers have come to expect as part of the value equation. From a customer's perspective, these expected services range from "unnoticed givens" to "looked for features." For example, customers of retail banks expect ATM access to their accounts as a given. They also expect bank statements, but look for and, most important,

Figure 3.6 **FedEx Growth Map—Later 1990s**

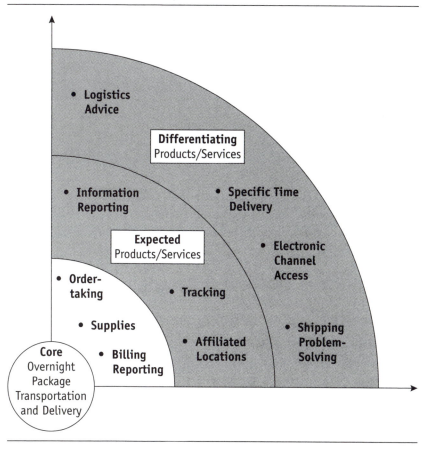

ask for extra features such as year-end consolidation, simplification across accounts, and daily account reconciliation they can access electronically. However, when buyers are evaluating one provider in comparison to another, they seldom ask about the givens and they treat the features as requirements on their selection checklist. In short, all competitors must provide these expected products and services. Innovations in this wave of the growth map have very short time windows of opportunity in terms of their impact on attracting new customers but can have significant impact on customer retention.

The third and final wave represents the leading edge of benefits desired by customers relative to the core offering. It provides the best opportunity for differentiation of one's business versus competition. As shown in Figure 3.6 (page 37), FedEx has now pushed into offering problem-solving help for shipping managers as well as providing its highly regarded logistics expertise for companies' internal logistics functions. Innovations in this wave help drive customer demand by creating new and stronger customer relationships.

This portrayal of the expected and differentiating benefit levels of a service is certainly not static in competitive markets. Competition will always act like gravity on a company's offerings to customers—pulling their perceived uniqueness down until they reach a point of parity with everyone else. To combat this, "be different" companies continually launch waves of new and unique value into the marketplace. And the greater the newness or the more revolutionary the efforts away from the core business of today, the greater the chance for accelerated growth. The growth map helps to pictorialize what customers need and how much value they place on new functionality and features that extend the benefits of the core offering.

Alternative Approaches to Accelerated Growth: Revolution or Evolution

To know when to focus "be different" efforts in a particular way, service providers must examine how a service offering and a company evolve during a market's life cycle. Often people ask: "Should we pursue revolution or evolution regarding our 'be different' efforts?" This is similar to the question regarding the Earth's development, "Should we believe the creation theory or the evolution theory?" The answer for either question is: both. God created the elements of the earth, and then they evolved. Creation or revolution always precedes evolution. Determining what "be different" strategies to apply to your organization at what time is simply about deciding if it's time for revolution or the next phase of evolution.

Regardless of its cycle of evolution, the goal for a service company is to create new things or "energy" that will enable it to shine brightly and distinctly in the minds of customers. This occurs by continuously pursuing "be different" strategies so that the benefits being offered to customers will not fade, degenerate into obscurity, or become perceived as a commodity.

Figure 3.7 depicts a framework that combines the type of benefits desired or needed by customers (in other words, *what* will be provided) with the time frame in which to prioritize "be different" efforts—the *when*.

Stage I—Invent Benefits

In Stage I of evolution, the primary objective is to be the first to start a new life cycle or create a market niche. In other words, invent or

Figure 3.7 **Evolution of a Service Market**

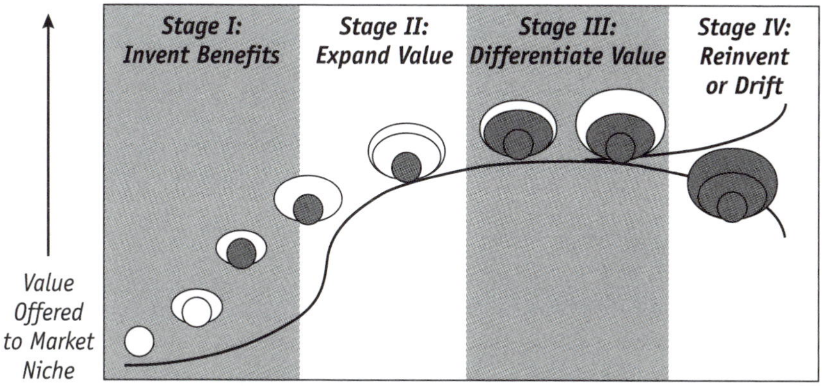

Note: *Shading in the novas shows the degree of commodity perception among customers*

reinvent the core offering. Naturally, this will also entail some necessary supplemental products and services to make it more appealing to the new buyers of this offering. This stage draws to a close when other competitors begin to provide similar core offerings with comparable and acceptable quality. The length of this stage varies according to the dynamics of each individual industry and market niche.

Stage II—Expand Value

Winners during evolution's Stage II are the first to create a pipeline of new and valued services. These services extend the core service offering and breathe new life into it. Typically, a Stage I market and/or service invention provides a lot of opportunity for expansion—new features, different bundles of features, new pricing structures, new delivery approaches, and the like. All of these can extend the life of the new offering and prop up gross margins. Unfortunately, they often are easily duplicated and quickly migrate to becoming expected products and services.

Stage III—Differentiate Value

When most competitors are now offering the full range of expected offerings, Stage III has begun. Stage III's objective is to be first to offer new differentiating products and services, the outer waves. The truly "be different" organization should be energized to push the edge of their growth map and offer nontraditional new offerings. Oftentimes Stage III is executed in conjunction with alliance partners who own breakthrough technologies. Also, it may focus on targeting new customer groups or new market categories.

Stage IV—Reinvent or Drift

Stage IV is the most dangerous one for a company pursuing a "be different" mind-set. The leaders that have grown with the business are very comfortable with running it and often prefer not to change dramatically. Customer relationships are solid and the competitive dynamics have stabilized such that growth (or lack thereof) appears fairly predictable. Although there is absolute perceived parity among the top competitors in the market niche, conservatism dictates to stay the course. There may be a slow decline of customers and margins, but it is hardly noticed. Breakthrough "be different" efforts and investments are nonexistent. Creativity has shut down and the organization is adrift, heading toward either an externally forced or self-imposed crisis. Whether it happens because of new management, Wall Street pressure, customer defections, new or global competitors, the threat of acquisition, or all of the above—the core offering will get redefined.

What drives company leaders and managers to pursue strategies that will enable their organizations to be revolutionarily different? It certainly starts with a goal to grow the organization dramatically. But there is also a less tangible factor at work. Sometimes, it is a fear of business failure. Sometimes, it is a desire to have an impact with customers. Still other times, it is an internal motivation to beat the competition. In all cases, the drive to be different requires a definitive mind-set toward inventing or creating value for customers that results in accelerated profitable growth. It requires harnessing the collective ingenuity of an organization to create new solutions to customer problems—and doing it in such a way that customers perceive unique and increased value being delivered relative to other providers. It is being an industry leader, not because of size, operational quality, or brand recognition, but because of a reputation for being a difference-maker, a partner, and a strategic problem-solver with customers.

Giving Customers a Different Experience

The greatest challenge for "be different" strategies is the need to be innovative with both the unique customer benefits a company delivers, as well as with *how* customers actually experience the service itself. For example, an innovative golf instructor who has a unique way for golfers to hit the ball farther may give lessons through the use of virtual reality technology rather than on an actual golf driving range. This would be a unique way for golfers to experience the service of golf instruction.

Service innovations have the most impact when both what is being offered and how it is being delivered are unique. How is this done? First, innovating what benefit a company provides to customers should track with the life cycle of the market niche and the natural evolution of differentiating attributes for the service the company is providing. Second, the customer experience—i.e., how the service is delivered—should also be different. To deliver a "different" customer experience, the company must focus on the intangible actions that create the promised experience. This goes counter to conventional wisdom (a major trap for many service organizations), which believes that a company must innovate the tangible aspects of the service in order to create value in the service experience. For example, bank customers may favor one bank over another because of the speed with which they can receive their cash when in the bank (i.e., the service experience). However, it would be rare to find a customer who selected a bank due to the sophistication of the cash drawer that enabled the bank representative to dispense cash faster.

For every type of service there is a different mix of intangible actions and tangible service enablers. Building on the framework from Chapter 1, Figure 3.8 (page 43) highlights the differences according to the type of service.

Across service industries, customers generally care little about the tangible items that help deliver the promised experience—they care about the experience itself. Service market leaders know a secret. The customer experience is everything, and the focus should be on differentiating the intangible actions that produce the experience. The tangible enablers are alluring mirages pretending to be valued by customers. Keep them behind the scenes where they belong and lose the mind-set that they are a differentiating investment. Tangible enablers should be automated, cost-reduced, streamlined for efficiency, and built upon proven technologies and approaches. Focus instead on the intangible actions in order to create a unique service experience— innovate the service process itself and innovate how people in your organization add value to the experience.

Conclusion

The quest by any organization to be different is a journey. It is a journey that should be ongoing but broken into specific strategies and actions for different time periods. For example, Microsoft set out many

Figure 3.8 **Intangibles and Tangibles of Various Services**

	Who or What Receives the Service?			
	People's Minds	**People's Bodies**	**Physical Assets**	**Intangible Assets**
Examples	• Consulting • Information services	• Restaurants • Passenger transportation	• Overnight mail • Car repair	• Insurance • Banking
Intangible Actions	• Converting raw data into information • Customer participation in analysis	• Employees' concern for safety and satisfaction • Customer's interaction with fellow customers	• Packages arriving undamaged • Customer being shown worn parts before repairs	• Increased solvency rating of insurance firm • Automatic sweep of cash into money market fund
Tangible Service Enablers	• Electronic database • Software analytical tools	• Wines in wine cellar • Technology embedded in locomotives	• Specially designed trucks • Diagnostic equipment	• Written policy • Sophisticated computer systems

years ago to be different by making personal computers easy to use by the average person. Their journey is ongoing and far from over. However, during rolling five-year periods of time, they have pursued specific strategies to distinguish themselves from the competitive landscape of the time. During the late 1990s, they have been on a course to take advantage of computer networks and communications to make personal computers more versatile and easier to use. Microsoft remains competitively different today because of its commitment to continually redefine and pursue "be different" strategies, and management's experience in what this journey brings over time: growth and profit margins.

But what really is the journey or process to be different? Managers give a variety of responses including:

"redefining our industry every five years"

"finding and exploiting new market niches before competitors do"

"finding an approach to satisfying our customers' needs in a totally unique way"

"creating breakthrough value for customers that keeps us ahead of our competitors" "creating things that our customers don't yet know they want"

"developing new services and products on an on-going basis"

A "be different" strategy is not about increasing your market share a few percentage points by taking business from competitors. Market share swapping is reserved for short-term marketing programs such as price reductions, trade deals, and sales incentives. If management thinks this is the only way to grow the business, then they should greatly downsize the growth-side ranks in the company and simply start acquiring competitors. Instead, a "be different" leader is about expanding the market niche or growing revenues per customer. It means creating new value and, in return, new growth—created growth versus engineered growth. Chapters 4–14 explain the specific step-wise strategies service companies can adopt to charter a "be different" course toward market leadership.

PART II

Dominating
Markets

CHAPTER 4

Learn to Say "No"

SERVICE MARKET LEADERS HAVE FOUND THAT success begins with limiting their focus and saying "No."

"No" to certain markets

"No" to some types of customers

"No" to certain categories of service offerings

"No" to some service levels

"No" to expansion into some geographies

"No" to certain growth opportunities

Bigger does not necessarily mean better. Bigger does not necessarily mean more competitive. And, most important, bigger often does not mean higher profitability.

Service companies often spread their resources too thinly across multiple areas of a market. They decline to rule out any opportunities for growth. This malady is rooted (1) in the sales-driven culture that believes any opportunity for a sale must be pursued, or (2) in an operations-driven culture that wants to spread its costs of doing business across as many markets as possible. Senior management frequently pursues the myth that customers truly want one-stop shopping across a broad range of services. Company mind-sets that encourage a lack of focus are especially prevalent in industries emerging from deregulation—such as telecommunications and utilities—where companies were once required to serve *all* customers and provide *one* (typically low) level of service. But history tells us that, over time, markets mature and divide into smaller niches, with new markets emerging to compete with or replace existing ones.

For example, when the overnight delivery market was first invented, the offerings in this market were limited to one basic level of service. As new competitors entered the market, they explored different dimensions of the market and started to specialize. Today, the market has since subdivided into what is now a variety of emphases:

- speed and precision of delivery (priority mail before 10:00 A.M., before 2:00 P.M., two-day delivery, etc.)
- geographic coverage (domestic versus international delivery)
- industry and company size (time-sensitive logistics industry, small businesses, etc.)
- convenience (package pickup versus drop-off)
- price sensitivity

While the overnight delivery market is now far too heterogeneous for one company to possibly dominate in its entirety, rest assured, some will try. But those likely to enjoy the greatest success will say "No."

Similarly, take a look at the energy marketplace. It used to be easy to identify a utility company as an entity that generated (or purchased), transported, and distributed electricity, gas, or both to a company or home. But as today's utility marketplace deregulates, it is evolving into multiple market niches where focused service providers will predominate. Some companies will concentrate on winning in the power generation arena through innovative, cost-effective supply strategies. Others will develop an expertise in the discipline of commodity trading and wholesale marketing of gas or electricity. Still others will specialize in the local energy distribution business—pipes and wires connected to customers' homes and businesses. Finally, some companies will direct their efforts toward delivering services that customers need to run their homes and businesses in a more cost-effective and energy-efficient way. Individual companies will simply not have the resources and expertise to dominate multiple market niches across a broad range of customer sets (e.g., large industrial, small business, residential), or across multiple geographies (e.g., regions, countries, continents). By 2005, the once "sleepy" and predictable utility industry will forever have changed, and a key requirement for market leadership will be focus—a difficult but necessary decision to say "No!" to being all things to all people.

In this chapter, more specific attention will be paid to the benefits of saying "No," alternative strategies for saying "No," and how to say "No." The chapter will also touch briefly on the potential downsides of becoming overly focused to the exclusion of change.

The Benefits of Saying "No"

The message is clear. While a single company might sell its offerings to a variety of market niches, how can it possibly focus on and keep up with changing dynamics simultaneously in *all* of those market niches? The answer is simple: they can't. However, service companies that concentrate on specific market niches reap the rewards of being a *focused service enterprise,* a concept that replaces the notion that the keys to profitability are to acquire as many customers as possible, to become the broad market share leader, to move down the experience curve, and to drive to the low-cost position. Instead, the new paradigm calls for delivering superior profits by concentrating on doing a few things extremely well for highly targeted segments of customers. Superior profitability is then realized through:

1. improved resource prioritization
2. increased operational efficiency and improved asset utilization
3. increased employee effectiveness
4. higher and more consistent service quality
5. increased ability to differentiate the company and its services

In turn, these five elements interact to create synergies that reduce operating costs, increase customer loyalty and retention, and, ultimately, improve profitability (Figure 4.1, page 50). Past research findings support the positive benefits that service companies reap by being focused (Davidow and Uttal 1989).

Figure 4.1 **Impact of Focus**

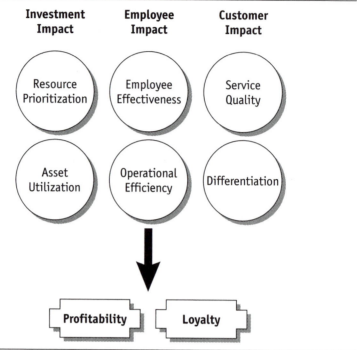

Improved Resource Prioritization

Focused service companies are better able to prioritize their growth opportunities and initiatives. Consequently, they tend to reap higher returns on their investments. Unfocused companies, on the other hand, apply too few resources against too many initiatives. They become unable to complete initiatives in a timely, cost-effective way.

Consider Minnegasco, a division of Reliant Energy that distributes gas in the Minneapolis area. A decade before energy deregulation came to the residential marketplace, Minnegasco foresaw that retaining residential customers would eventually require service far above and beyond simply delivering gas to the home. The company could have invested in a lot of different initiatives—to increase operating efficiency, expand geographic coverage, provide alternative energy sources, etc. But they focused on becoming an outstanding home-service provider. With this singular vision, Minnegasco developed new products and services to meet residential customers' needs beyond gas distribution. They started with furnace maintenance and repair. Imagine the importance to customers of having heat in the middle of a Minnesota winter!

- Minnegasco invested in hiring and training their own dedicated staff of employees who could maintain and repair customers' furnaces, water heaters, and a variety of other major household appliances.
- They invested in assets and created processes to receive calls from customers, dispatch service employees, manage parts inventory, and deliver home services.
- They tracked service quality and put mechanisms in place to consistently improve it. They created a "good night's sleep" service guarantee that offered a free hotel stay if a customer's furnace could not be repaired the same day.

One family actually had its furnace go out on a subzero night in Minneapolis. Minnegasco was there in fifteen minutes and the furnace was operating again within thirty minutes after the initial telephone call.

Minnegasco now dominates this niche market. Even Sears Home-Central takes a backseat in Minnegasco's territory. Most important, Minnegasco's customers give a very consistent message—they won't take their gas business elsewhere, even in a competitive marketplace. Why? Because Minnegasco had the focus and foresight to make the right investments. They have locked customers in, and they are, arguably, a decade ahead of any competitor.

Increased Operational Efficiency and Improved Asset Utilization

Service companies that operate under a focused-enterprise approach generate operational efficiencies. First, they can strip away unnecessary costs and concentrate only on activities that their target customers truly value. Second, service employees who repeatedly perform similar functions over time become more efficient, thereby reducing the labor costs associated with delivering the service. Third, focused service companies can often realize higher utilization of their assets due to having less idle capacity, while ensuring that their investments are best suited to the requirements of the markets they serve. Overall, these three characteristics of focused service companies contribute to lower operating costs relative to less-focused competitors.

For example, a medical practice specializing in performing ultrasounds for pregnant women will achieve certain operational efficiencies that a general-purpose OB-GYN practice cannot. Among such efficiencies are the following:

- They can precisely target investments in staff, office space, equipment, supplies, etc. that suit only the specific needs of ultrasound patients. There is no need for investment in expensive beds that perform other functions, in laboratory testing equipment, or in hiring nurses and technicians with expertise beyond ultrasounds.
- They have more efficient patient processing because employees are exceedingly skilled at setting up, performing, and reading ultrasounds.
- They have higher utilization of expensive ultrasound equipment, resulting in lower per-transaction costs of using the equipment. The cost of these fixed assets is spread over more patients.

Similarly, Southwest Airlines has been able to establish efficient operations by concentrating on short-haul routes and budget-conscious travelers. Southwest's focus enables them to fly a fleet comprised solely of Boeing 737s. An obvious benefit is the significant reduction in parts inventories. Labor costs are also lower for flight crews and for maintenance and gate check-in personnel due to (1) their familiarity with the planes, (2) reduced training costs, and (3) lower labor requirements overall for 737s relative to other planes. Asset utilization is high because Southwest has been able to strip out the costs and time associated with assigned seating. The results—significantly faster turnaround times at the gate. These operational efficiencies add up and have helped Southwest achieve an unmatched record of consistent profit performance in a traditionally cyclical industry.

Increased Employee Effectiveness

At the heart of a service company are the customer-contact personnel who deliver the service experience. Companies that operate with a focused service enterprise approach can achieve increased employee effectiveness. Why? Because focus enables better employee selection, training, and retention. Focused companies typically hire in a narrower range of job positions with accurate job descriptions. This enables recruiters to quickly learn the characteristics of ideal candidates and to develop even more accurate job descriptions that further improve employee selection. In addition, a narrower range of positions allows training to be tailored, appropriate cross training to be offered, and more in-depth training to be delivered. The result: development of in-depth, specialized skills.

Consider the hiring and training requirements for Jiffy Lube versus general auto repair shops. Jiffy Lube creates a much tighter specification for the type of individual they need. This results in a selection process that is targeted and cost-effective. Similarly, they offer cross training that provides repair technicians with the ability to perform additional store functions. This opportunity adds greater interest to the technicians' jobs and reduces overall store costs. Jiffy Lube also offers specialized training for their narrower range of service offerings. All of these circumstances contribute to improved employee effectiveness. Contrast this to a general repair shop, where one day a technician is replacing brakes on a Honda and the next day performing a tune-up on a Chevrolet. In the early 1990s, a large automotive repair chain was experiencing an average of one "oil out" per day. An oil out occurs during an oil change when oil is removed from the engine, but accidentally not replaced with new oil. The result is a catastrophic seizure of pistons, crankshaft, and valves. The engine must be replaced—quite an expensive error. Although an oil change is a relatively simple procedure, the complexity involved with managing a broad range of service offerings reduces employee effectiveness and can result in costly mistakes.

Finally, focused service enterprises benefit from having specialists who develop unique expertise that enables them to be more effective with and to deliver greater value to customers. With repetition comes not only efficiency but also expertise. Recall the ultrasound technician who performs five to ten procedures per day, five days per week. In a relatively short period of time, that person unquestionably develops greater expertise in conducting, reading, interpreting, and delivering the results of an ultrasound than does the typical OB-GYN doctor, even one who has been practicing for years. This type of unique expertise is valued by customers and will be remembered and passed on to countless others seeking the same service.

Higher and More Consistent Service Quality

Companies that operate as a focused service enterprise typically achieve higher and more consistent levels of service quality for four reasons:

1. They have a better understanding of the customer's specific requirements and expectations because the company can focus its research efforts on a narrower set of topics and customers. When understood and acted upon across the organization (e.g., service development, marketing, operations, customer service), greater application of customer insights can lead to improved service quality.

2. The company can set tighter quality specifications based on this improved understanding of the customer. Tighter specifications, in conjunction with improved resource prioritization, enable focused companies to design and develop services that are inherently more reliable (e.g., avoiding oil outs altogether) and deliver a more consistent service experience.

3. As previously mentioned, better employee selection and improved training permit a service to be delivered at specific quality levels. Employees also tend to develop unique expertise over time, enabling an improved ability to influence customer perceptions and be more responsive to customer needs. In particular, employees become more effective in anticipating and responding to customer problems and complaints.

4. The range of customer expectations may be narrower and more in line with the company's service delivery capabilities. For example, the communication materials of focused service enterprises can be precisely targeted and thereby more effective. The result: the com-

pany attracts customers who most likely understand and desire the experience the company will deliver.

In summary, focused companies have a greater likelihood of understanding and meeting customer expectations and of managing customer perceptions. They are more capable of delivering consistently high-quality service over time. And higher levels of service quality ultimately translate into positive word of mouth, greater customer loyalty, and increased profitability.

Increased Ability to Differentiate the Company and Its Services

A final benefit of operating a focused service enterprise is an increased ability to differentiate the company and its services, a highly desirable result that can lead to premium pricing and higher profits. Consumer behavior research shows that people only remember and consider a handful of companies in any given category of products or services. Try the test yourself. What companies would you consider for the following services: long-distance telephone, rental cars, management consulting, airlines, overnight mail, car insurance, discount retail clothing? Who would you select? In each case, most people:

(1) quickly develop a short list of three to five companies they would consider

(2) make their selection based on the company that best meets their individual set of needs at a particular point in time

Getting on a customer's short list requires awareness of the brand. But becoming the company of choice only occurs when you deliver a meaningful point of difference and demonstrate that point of difference to customers through communication and action. Companies that try to stand for too many things end up standing for nothing and are unable to demonstrate a compelling point of difference. On the contrary, focused service enterprises can better demonstrate their inherent advantages and, therefore, can charge a price premium even while achieving higher levels of customer retention. The bottom line is higher profitability.

Contrast the Internet bookseller Amazon.com with large national book chains like Borders and Barnes & Noble. With Amazon's sole emphasis being the Internet domain, Amazon learns faster and moves quicker than the larger, less-focused competitors. Customer needs, expectations, and behaviors are different on the Internet, and Amazon has responded by creating offerings and services tailored to address the Internet's unique characteristics. Not only have they managed to become one of the best-known brands on the World Wide Web (both on- and off-line), Amazon has created a meaningful point of difference for the customer—one place to go to search, research, purchase, mail, and comment on the largest selection of books. The large, traditional booksellers are scrambling to catch up, but Amazon remains several steps ahead.

So why focus a service company? Rather than pursuing a goal of sheer size, the goal should be to *dominate* a series of market niches and not try to be all things to all types of customers. Only by choosing, pursuing, and dominating a select number of niches can a service company sustain superior profitability over time. This enables the focused service company to direct its resources and efforts in ways that less-focused competitors cannot match with the same level of intensity or speed.

Now that some of the benefits of saying "No" have been discussed and demonstrated, let's turn to the when and where of saying "No."

Alternative Strategies for Saying "No"

Far too many service companies have avoided focus in the name of providing a one-stop shop for customers, only to find out that either customers don't care or the complexity and costs are overwhelming. Conversely, some service companies have successfully employed a variety of approaches for concentrating their businesses. Specifically, service companies can select from among the following six alternative focus strategies:

- Lines of business
- Service offerings
- Benefits delivered
- Geographies served

- Channels of access used
- Types of customers served

Oftentimes, companies employ several of these strategies simultaneously. The success requirements and potential pitfalls differ significantly for each strategy. In addition, the circumstances that would lead a company to select one or more of these strategies tend to be related to company-specific factors (e.g., size, geographic coverage, expertise, resources available, etc.) or to market-specific factors (e.g., market maturity, number of competitors and their areas of concentration, emerging customer needs, etc.). The criteria for selecting the appropriate focus strategies will be discussed under "How to Say 'No.'"

Focusing the Lines of Business

The first strategy is to limit the company's lines of business or markets served. Typically, each additional line of business requires new expertise and people skills, information systems, internal processes, regulatory knowledge, distribution channels, and marketing communication approaches—as well as a different business model for generating revenues and profits. Each additional line of business also requires two scarce resources—management attention and investment dollars. For example, several banks have decided to focus solely on corporate customers and, thereby, to exit the retail banking business (or vice versa). Similarly, some insurance companies have opted to focus on the property and casualty insurance markets and exit the health insurance market (or vice versa).

In the 1990s, Waste Management tried to become the one-stop shop for an entire range of services in the areas of environmental consulting, engineering, and chemical and solid waste hauling and disposal. To put all the necessary pieces together, they purchased a variety of companies. The difficulty Waste Management encountered came in trying to:

- integrate the various companies' sales forces, operations, customer service organizations, information systems, and internal processes
- create a cohesive culture for the parent company while still recognizing the uniqueness of each operating unit

- create an understandable and compelling brand identity
- bring together the portfolio of services in a way that made sense to customers

But a company with such a diverse set of offerings proved to be largely unmanageable. Waste Management's performance has trailed that of the overall stock market. By the late 1990s, it had decided to divest itself of several lines of business and merge with another large waste services provider in an attempt to refocus on their original core business.

Focusing the Service Offerings

A second focus strategy is to limit the number and type of service offerings and become a specialist with a limited menu. This approach can be effective from two different perspectives:

1. Some companies that employ the limited menu strategy can develop deep levels of expertise and, thereby, charge a price premium for their services. For example, a real estate tax specialist has unique expertise and can typically charge more for services than a general tax accountant. Customers who have a need for and value this niche expertise are willing to pay a premium to reduce their overall tax bill, insure compliance with government tax codes, and reduce the risk of an audit.

2. A limited menu strategy can enable companies to "cherry pick" high-profit margin services. If a company can develop a tailored, efficient service delivery process for a limited range of offerings, it may be able to provide a price discount and deliver higher-quality results (due to a singular focus), while still reaping superior profits. Most veterinarians, for example, make a substantial profit on routine, annual procedures such as heartworm tests and on heartworm medication. These procedures and products subsidize the more complex diagnoses and treatments that tend to occur infrequently and are unpredictable. For these reasons, some of the national pet supply superstores are considering offering a limited menu of veterinary services in their stores, concentrating on the more routine, recurring, highly profitable ones. By offering a limited menu of routine services and spreading the fixed occupancy costs over the entire store, these pet superstores can pro-

vide certain veterinary services at a significant discount relative to a veterinary clinic. This trend threatens traditional veterinarians who depend on routine services to keep customers coming back on a regular basis, thereby threatening a substantial source of profits.

Pursuing a focused service offering strategy requires either a profound, continuously deepening expertise (e.g., real estate tax accounting expertise) or a low-cost approach to service operations (e.g., routine veterinary services). In both instances, the unique expertise or low-cost operating approach must be sustainable over time. Otherwise, the selected areas of focus will be quickly replicated in the marketplace.

Focusing the Benefits Delivered

The third focus strategy is to offer a limited range of benefits—usually across a fairly broad range of services. Typically, this strategy is employed along with fixing attention on a set of customers who place high value on the derived benefits. The goal is to own a benefit in the mind of customers and then to offer that benefit to them across a broad range of related services.

Companies in many service industries focus on the benefit of speed, which can be an important point of difference in such widely divergent industries as priority overnight mail and pizza delivery. Some corporations are extremely time-sensitive because downtime on their production line can cost hundreds of thousands of dollars per hour. W.W. Grainger is focused on delivering the benefit of time—they distribute a very broad range of parts and end products to companies that need these items immediately. Time-sensitive companies are willing to pay a premium to have parts delivered quickly, because this enables them to minimize production downtime.

The key to successfully implementing a benefit-focus strategy is developing some unique capability that delivers the desired benefit, can be leveraged across a relatively broad set of service offerings, and cannot easily be replicated. For example, a company might invest in a technology that gives it an advantage (fast-cooking ovens), a distribution system that is expensive to duplicate (an overnight mail hub in Memphis, Tennessee), an analytical process that is proprietary (a model for measuring portfolio risk), or a patented procedure (laser eye surgery).

Focusing the Geographies Served

A fourth focus strategy is to limit the company's geographic coverage to a city, state, region, country, continent, etc. However, as communications have become faster and less expensive and as global trade barriers have been reduced, this focus strategy has become viable only when one or more of the following situations are present:

- Significant, sustainable barriers to geographic expansion exist, such as regulatory environment or significant capital investment requirements.
- Customer needs vary significantly across different geographies and continue to evolve in different directions.
- Economies of scale cannot be realized either in terms of a company's ability to communicate across geographic areas to leverage mass-market advertising costs or to spread fixed investments and internal operating costs.
- Customers operate in a geographically limited area, or purchase decision authority resides in each geographic area (applicable for business-to-business services).
- A major purchase criteria is that the company be locally owned or operated (although this factor can sometimes be overcome through creative branding or ownership structures).

Across many different service industries, one traditional area of opportunity for geographic focus is small business. Historically, small businesses tend to be ignored by large, national service providers because they represent minimal revenue per customer. But several conditions can make small businesses an attractive market for a geographically focused service provider, as small businesses often:

- have different needs than large and mid-sized companies
- operate in a limited geographic area
- make purchase decisions on a local basis
- are less sophisticated in their decision-making processes
- are more reputation and brand conscious

In some service industries, geographically focused companies can create consortia or alliances with similar companies in other geographic areas to create the benefits of scale while retaining the benefits of local customer intimacy. Local and regional travel agencies are forming consortia that enable them to create stronger purchasing power with airlines, hotels, and rental car companies. This, in turn, allows them to provide very competitive rates to customers. Such consortia are also sharing technology, thereby allowing large, fixed investments to be spread over many small companies. The consortia approach enables each travel agency to operate more cost-effectively, provide competitive rates, and concentrate on local customer service.

Focusing the Channels of Access

A fifth focus strategy is to limit the types of channels that a customer may use to access the service provider. The most common types of access channels are retail stores, telephone, mail, fax, electronic access (Internet, automated teller machines), and multimedia (videoconference, TV). While retail store channels offer the very significant benefit of direct customer contact, other channels tend to be less expensive to establish and maintain. Beyond cost considerations, customer expectations vary for each access channel, as do customer behaviors. For example, one company developing services for a combined television, telephone, and Internet access device found that people's expectations for Internet response time were extremely high. That is because customers perceived they were accessing the services through their television (which has very quick response time), rather than through a computer (which tends to have a slower response time). As with other focus strategies, this one is often employed along with a concentration on specific segments of customers that prefer a certain type of access channel or are willing to accept the trade-off of lesser service levels for reduced costs.

The key conditions to consider when employing a focused access channel strategy are as follows:

- one-time and ongoing costs of operating the access channel
- target segments of customers served and their needs, expectations, and behaviors with the access channel
- unique benefits that can be delivered through each channel, and the ability to uniquely or more cost-effectively serve target customers' needs

- limitations of the access channel, and relative importance of these limitations to targeted customers
- speed with which customers will adopt that method of access (for newer access channels), and the company's ability to influence that access method
- ability to offer future products and services through the access channel, and the range of products and services that could be offered

As mentioned earlier, Amazon.com on the Internet uses a focused access channel strategy to redefine the way customers buy books. Because Amazon is not saddled with huge investments in and ongoing expenditures associated with retail bookstores, they can cost-effectively compete in offering their initial core product—books. They have worked hard to really understand the needs, expectations, and behaviors of Internet shoppers. They pay very close attention to the service experience that their customers receive, continually modifying the user interface to meet the evolving needs of their customers. Amazon has developed new Internet services to focus on the expanded needs of convenience, speed, information, personalization, and book reviews, as well as the unique needs of certain purchase occasions such as gift giving. In short, Amazon is maximizing the advantages of the Internet access channel for their target customers in a way that is extremely difficult for competitors to match.

Focusing the Types of Customers Served

The final focus strategy for a company is to limit the customers served. We'll talk in depth about this strategy in the next chapter because selection of customer segments is a core element of every focus strategy. Companies should continuously strive to identify underserved sets of customers and select segments where it can use existing capabilities or acquire new capabilities to satisfy customer needs and expectations in a superior, sustainable way.

The real power of these six focus strategies comes from applying several of them in concert, selecting multiple market niches to pursue, and building the internal capabilities that enable the company to cost-effectively serve multiple niches. The next section will address the creative, iterative, ongoing process of determining which niche opportunities to serve.

How to Say "No"

All six of the focus strategies require insight and analysis to answer the fundamental question: "Which strategies should I pursue, and, within each strategy, which niche opportunities should I select and which ones should I ignore?"

The principal goal should be to identify certain niches that the company can dominate. To achieve this goal, a company should take the following two steps (Figure 4.2):

Step 1: Gather and Analyze Relevant Information

• **Assess internal capabilities.** Look within each of the functional areas of the company and then across these functions to assess internal processes, technologies, people expertise, facilities, service offerings, cost structure, responsiveness to customer needs, and the like. The key is to identify those capabilities that are in some way either unique or superior to the competition.

Figure 4.2 Overview Approach for Saying "No"

Step 1 Gather and Analyze Relevant Information	Step 2 Identify, Prioritize, and Select Opportunities
• Assess internal capabilities • Identify potential markets served • Identify customer segments • Identify and profile competitors • Determine unmet customer needs	• Identify pockets of opportunity • Find the intersection • Develop alternative focus strategies to dominate niches • Evaluate and select optimal strategies

- **Identify potential markets served.** A market is a set of customers who are trying to fulfill a specific function. You know you've crossed markets when some combination of the customer needs, buyers, purchase criteria and process, types of products or services offered, and competition have changed.
- **Identify customer segments.** Within each market, segment the customers based on different needs, attitudes, behaviors, and channels of access used (See Chapter 5 for more details on this process). If the company is already serving certain customer segments, it can also determine the current cost to serve each segment.
- **Identify and profile competitors.** Within each market, identify competitors' current positionings, direction, offerings, capabilities, and unique advantages.
- **Determine unmet customer needs.** Within each customer segment, determine customer needs that are: fully satisfied and met, only partially met, unmet, or unknown (emerging).

The detailed process for completing many of these activities has been well-documented in a variety of marketing strategy books. The real challenges are determining underserved or emerging customer needs, and then applying all of the information to make well-informed strategic decisions (Step 2 of the process). Much more will be presented in Chapter 9 on the topic of uncovering customer needs. For now, suffice it to say that customers have difficulty articulating their needs. On the other hand, they tend to be quite vocal about their problems, likes and dislikes, frustrations, emotions, experiences, wishes, usage and perceptions of existing products and services, and perceptions of companies providing services. From this vocalization can come a wealth of information for determining customer needs. But how do you get customers to talk about their unknown needs? You can't. To uncover unknown needs requires creative approaches to accomplishing the following:

- educate customers about a potential "future state"
- create scenarios where customers can realistically put themselves into this future state
- give customers "if-then" (hypothetical) choices to determine how they would behave under various conditions or given certain options

- probe as to why customers selected the hypothetical options they did, what benefits these options would provide, and why these benefits would be important

Step 2: Identify, Prioritize, and Select Opportunities

- **Identify pockets of opportunity.** Look for the areas where: (a) the company has unique strengths, (b) competitors are weaker, and (c) customer needs are underserved or emerging;
- **Find the intersection.** High-potential opportunities are found at the intersection of the above three areas.
- **Develop alternative focus strategies to dominate niches.** Generate alternative combinations of the six strategies for saying "No" to see which ones will enable the company to dominate certain niches. Here's the key: these should not be generic strategies often promoted by various consultants and academics and often used by product companies. Generic strategies oversimplify the issues for service companies, and companies become deceived into thinking they can achieve sustained market leadership by adopting generic strategies such as:

- operational excellence, customer intimacy, or product leadership
- leader, challenger, follower, or nicher
- innovator, second-but-better, imitator, or laggard

Service companies must develop leadership strategies that have as their starting point a knowledge of specific market and customer niches that is much better than any of their competitors'. Then, they must thoughtfully build and tailor operations and delivery for the specific purpose of serving those niches. A service market leader strives simultaneously to achieve low-cost operations, valued services and products, and close customer relationships within selected niches. This approach leads to sustained market leadership for service companies. Chapters 8–15 will provide much more detail on "how" to make this happen.

- **Evaluate and select the optimal strategies.** Develop criteria and evaluate each of the alternative strategies. Key evaluation criteria should include:

✓ Uniqueness—how difficult is it for competitors to replicate the strategy?

✓ Longevity—how well does the strategy fit with future trends, customer needs, and market changes?

✓ Efficiency—how efficiently can the internal infrastructure be leveraged across multiple niches using this strategy?

✓ Relative advantage—what advantages could the company have (or could it create) in pursuing this strategy vis-à-vis competitors?

✓ Profitability—does the strategy provide opportunities to generate adequate size of and growth in profits?

The Potential Dark Side of Focus

Remember the opening statement of this chapter: all defined markets ultimately mature and divide, and new markets emerge to replace or compete with existing ones. Leading service companies are nimble enough to create new opportunities, pursue new attractive niches, reinvent themselves, exit unprofitable territory, and the like. There are inherent risks in not doing so:

• You define your business too narrowly, and new competitors make it obsolete or relegate it to low-profit areas. A classic example can be found in the railroad industry. Many companies defined their businesses too narrowly by focusing solely on this one mode of transportation. Consequently, these railroad companies missed opportunities and were surpassed by others that defined their businesses more broadly as transportation—rather than railroads.

• Competitors develop a superior approach, and your focused offerings, benefits, or access channels are no longer competitive or, worse, become obsolete. For example, what offerings will the library of the future need to provide to be useful and "competitive" in the digital age? Certainly more than a storage and retrieval warehouse for printed material.

• Decision making shifts to a different buyer (e.g., centralized purchasing vs. local purchase authority), and the company is positioned with the wrong buyer.

• New technologies change the investment requirements, reduce entry barriers, or change the relative cost competitiveness of your current business.

Conclusion

Focus. That's the name of the game for service market leaders. But not without some peripheral vision. You have looked at the benefits of saying "No," alternative strategies for doing so, and the various ways to go about it. You have also learned there is a potential dark side if you proceed with blinders on. So, should you reinvent and cannibalize your existing markets and services offerings? Chapter 14 will provide insights on reinventing your company. As the saying goes, "It's better to keep the cannibal in the family." And this is especially true for service companies that chart a course to become a focused service enterprise.

CHAPTER 5

Be Number One with the Right Customers

To become dominant market leaders, service companies need to be the number one provider of choice with the most-profitable customer segments. They must dominate specific segments of customers. Recognizing a dominant market leader is simple—for their target customers, they consistently are the first provider to come to mind and the first to be selected. Customers go out of their way, and often pay more, to do business with them. Ultimately the goal should be to achieve 50 percent share or more of all purchases made by the targeted customers.

However, most service companies have a strong desire to be all things to all customers. Companies in the "all things to all customers" trap can't say "No" to any groups of customers. After all, how can you say "No" when you haven't met next month's or next quarter's sales goal? In your company, have you heard employees say:

"Customers are leaving us because our prices are too high."
"Customers cannot tell the difference between us and our competitors."
"All our competitors offer the same level of quality that we offer."
"We need to lower our prices to remain competitive."

If you have, then your company may have fallen into the "all things to all customers" trap. Customers are indifferent toward you relative to the competition, and they make purchase decisions solely based on price.

How does a service company get into this situation? It starts when the company has not carefully chosen segments of customers that it wants to attract. Over time, lack of focus on the needs of particular customer segments results in average performance across all segments. Unable to meet the specific needs of any particular customers, "all things to all customers" companies tend to perform marginally well in meeting the needs of all customers. They may hit a few customer "hot buttons" and generate enough sales and profits to stay in business. However, "all things to all customers" service companies do not distinguish themselves sufficiently with any particular customer segments. In the end, they cannot generate superior profits.

Think about the last time that you selected a new insurance company for your home or automobile. You probably turned to the Yellow Pages and called three of the top insurance companies, like Allstate, State Farm, and Farmers Insurance. After describing your circumstances, you asked them each to give you a quote and to tell you why you should select their company. Honestly, could you tell the difference between any of these companies? Did you have any reason to select one of them other than on the basis of price? Did any of them seem to be unique in any way? Did any of them try to understand and address your particular needs? Probably not. This same scenario occurs in dozens of service industries.

On the contrary, how did Enterprise become the number-one car rental company in the United States? They became number one with the right customers. Enterprise decided to avoid the highly competitive market for business travelers and, instead, to focus on the underserved market of customers needing a rental car while theirs is being repaired (either due to an accident or mechanical problem). Enterprise's typical facility is not located near airports where business travelers look for rental cars. Rather, their facilities are conveniently located for their target customers—in neighborhoods, near a variety of car repair shops. Furthermore, Enterprise knows their target customer has no way to get to a rental car facility (their car is being repaired). So they will deliver a car right to the customer—either to the repair shop or to the customer's home. When finished, Enterprise offers to pick up the rental car at the customer's home or the repair shop.

A business traveler may find Enterprise inconvenient, but a person whose car is being repaired thinks the world of them. Fundamentally, Enterprise has carefully selected its customers and then tailored every aspect of the company so it can cost-effectively address the needs of those target customers in a unique way.

Attracting the "Right" Customers

How do you get out of the "all things to all customers" pitfall that results in unsatisfactory profitability? Chapters 6 through 11 offer specific strategies. However, improving profitability starts with selecting the right areas of focus (Chapter 4) and being number one with the "right" customers. Service companies must narrow the target customer segments served, and select the "right" ones to pursue. By saying "No," a company should not necessarily refuse to serve particular segments of customers (although this is possible in some service industries). Rather, service companies can use six mechanisms to encourage the "right" customers and discourage the "wrong" customers:

1. *Communicate only in places where your target customer will see you.* One way of reaching frequent business travelers is to advertise in in-flight magazines. The next time you travel, open up the in-flight magazine and count the number of calling card advertisements. These companies are fighting a war over the frequent business traveler, and they know where to reach this target customer.

2. *Offer different levels of service for different types of customers.* Based on a customer's average monthly long-distance bill and the "newness" of their account, AT&T routes customers to different customer service representatives. If a customer has a history of loyalty to AT&T or has relatively high monthly long-distance bills, they will wait in a shorter queue and be routed to an experienced customer service agent. The major accounting firms take a similar approach. Corporations (large or small) that are willing to purchase multiple services on an ongoing basis from one accounting firm, rather than dividing their business across several firms, tend to receive dedicated account

teams and priority service levels. On the other hand, corporations that purchase services infrequently, purchase only a limited menu of services, or divide their purchases among several different firms simply don't get the same level of attention and priority.

3. *Offer different pricing for different types of customers.* A few years ago, First Chicago/NBD bank changed their pricing so that customers who kept low monthly balances would have to pay each time they visited a teller, or could use an ATM at no charge. First Chicago had uncovered the fact that a lot of small, unprofitable customers were driving up company costs and increasing the teller wait times for other customers. After receiving some initial negative publicity, First Chicago's bold move now appears to have paid off. They have encouraged less profitable customers to use a more efficient delivery system (the ATM network) or have driven unprofitable customers to the competition.

4. *Set expectations in advance and tailor the services and environment for your target customer.* Southwest Airlines does not try to attract business customers who require comforts such as first-class seating, preassigned seating, or full meal service. They eliminate these expectations up front and then tailor their services and the gate experience to a very different set of customers with different needs. For example, Southwest targets customers who are flying as an alternative to driving or to not taking a trip at all. Southwest also pursues small-business customers and lower and middle managers who are more concerned about reasonable fares than comfortable seats. Southwest actually discourages customers whose expectations don't fit their model.

5. *Provide more convenient access for target customers.* Locations of facilities, toll-free vs. toll phone access, pickup and delivery, and Internet access are different approaches that service companies can use to make it more (or less) convenient for certain types of customers.

6. *Prescreen customers and accept only those that meet certain criteria.* For example, the Shouldice Hospital in Toronto specializes in hernia operations and promises a quick recovery. In order to fulfill this promise, they prescreen patients for overall good health and for a specific type of hernia that is less complex. Local anesthesia and postoperative exercise are crucial elements to delivering the quick-recovery

promise. Therefore, Shouldice selects those customers who are appropriate candidates for their business model. As a result, the hospital is highly successful in fulfilling its quick-recovery promise.

Why is it so critical for service companies to attract the right customers? Remember that service experiences are intangible. Because experiences are intangible, customer expectations can vary greatly. Also, delivery against those expectations can be highly variable. By attracting the right customers, service companies can more effectively:

- manage customers' expectations
- tailor their delivery to meet or exceed those expectations
- manage customer perceptions of the service experience they received

Ultimately, service companies that attract the right customers can consistently deliver superior experiences—which translates into customers who are profitable and loyal.

Segmenting Service Markets

The process of segmenting service markets is a six-step approach (Figure 5.1, page 74):

1. Identify different needs, attitudes, behaviors, and demographics across a variety of potential customers.
2. Identify distinct segments of customers with similar purchase behaviors.
3. Create a profile describing each segment.
4. Size each segment.
5. Select the target segments.
6. Develop approaches for reaching target customers.

The ultimate goal is to select customer segments that the company can dominate, then tailor all aspects of the organization and its services to be number one with the "right" customers. To better illustrate this process, the following section contains a hypothetical segmentation of the overnight delivery market for corporate customers.

Figure 5.1 **Approach to Segmenting Service Markets**

1. Research
Collect responses to research on needs, attitudes,
behaviors, and demographics

↓

2. Analysis
Identify distinct customer segments who appear similar

↓

3. Segment Profiling
Define and describe segments based on demographics and other
information useful for target marketing

↓

4. Segment Sizing
Estimate the size of each segment by percentage of population
and revenue potential

↓

5. Segment Selection
Apply criteria and select most attractive segments

↓

6. Reaching the Segments
Develop strategies for reaching segments using various tools

Source: Nielson/Vantis International

Step 1: Identify Different Customer Needs, Attitudes, Behaviors, and Demographics

The first step in segmenting service markets is to develop a comprehensive set of customer needs, attitudes, behaviors, and demographic characteristics across a representative cross section of all potential customers. Most companies only focus on demographics (e.g., customer size, location, industry) and behaviors (e.g., frequency and amount of purchases). In service markets, a company needs to capture all four of these dimensions in order to accurately group customers into different segments where customers within each segment have similar purchase behaviors. Only then will the company be able to reach these customers in cost-effective ways.

Customer needs are requirements or desires that motivate the use of a particular service. They are often expressed as benefits the customer is looking for or expecting. Two aspects of customer needs that are unique to service markets are:

1. The complexity of the customer's needs. For example, multinational companies have much more complex travel requirements than U.S.–only companies.
2. The importance of a particular service to the customer or the customer's business. For example, production-intensive companies need timely delivery of parts to keep factories running.

In the overnight delivery market, customers may have a different intensity of need for requirements such as:

a. speed and precision of delivery (same-day, next-day, two-day, etc.)
b. geographic coverage
c. convenience of pick-up and drop-off
d. on-time reliability
e. delivery days (weekdays, Saturday, Sunday)
f. tracking of packages
g. size of packages
h. centralized billing

Customer attitudes are the beliefs and preferences of a particular customer. Attitudes include preferences toward certain brands or services as well as beliefs about what is important to that individual. Two unique attitudes to look for in service markets are:

1. The propensity to be "reactive" versus "proactive" in seeking services. For example, attitudes toward automotive repair or medical services may be reactive: wait until there is a problem; or proactive: perform preventive activities to avoid a problem.
2. The attitude toward establishing longer-term, integrated partnerships with a few service partners versus shorter-term, arms-length vendor relationships with a variety of service vendors.

For example, attitudes toward commercial lenders vary significantly. Some companies view their lender as an integral financial partner in their business and select a lender based on a wide variety of characteristics such as service levels, breadth of service offerings, etc. Others view their lender as a vendor of a commodity service and are more likely to select a lender solely on the basis of price.

Customer attitudes in the overnight delivery market might be assessed on the following dimensions:

a. beliefs about different brands of overnight delivery services
b. preferences for different overnight delivery companies
c. attitudes toward saving money
d. attitudes toward risk tolerance (e.g., guaranteed delivery)
e. attitudes toward customer service

Customer behaviors are specific actions customers have taken that can be tracked or measured. Included are:

- past products or services purchased
- average monthly usage levels of certain services
- propensity to switch service providers (e.g., loyalty)
- memberships in certain types of organizations
- subscriptions to certain magazines
- use of certain distribution channels, access methods, or shopping outlets

One unique behavior to look for in service markets is the inclination of certain customers to "do it themselves" versus "hire someone to do it for them." This is a critical dimension to investigate when segmenting business-to-business service markets such as information technology services, real estate services, and consulting services.

In the overnight delivery market, customer behaviors might include:

a. switching across different providers
b. degree to which selection of an overnight delivery company is centralized or decentralized

c. number of packages sent each month, by speed of delivery required
d. most frequent locations mailed to
e. types of items sent by overnight delivery
f. subscription to certain publications
g. membership in certain associations
h. purchase and use of related services (fax behavior, videoconferencing usage, travel patterns, etc.)

Customer demographics are characteristics typically available to the public and commonly tracked for the purposes of classifying customers. In consumer markets these might include age, income, household size, ethnicity, and geographic location. In the overnight delivery market for corporate customers, important demographic characteristics might include:

a. company revenues
b. number of employees
c. number of locations
d. primary industry classification of their business
e. locations of customers served
f. percent of business in international markets

This first step in understanding customer needs, attitudes, behaviors, and demographics is the most critical one in segmenting service markets. If a company doesn't thoroughly understand the breadth and depth of each of these dimensions, their segmentation will ultimately be flawed. The most effective approach for developing a comprehensive list of customer needs, attitudes, behaviors, and demographics is talking with customers in an open-ended way. This can be done through one-on-one interviews, small-group discussions (such as focus groups), observing customer behaviors, and other qualitative research methods. The most common mistake companies make at this stage is to jump right into conducting quantitative research prior to really understanding their customers along multiple dimensions. If a company misses an important dimension that explains customer purchase behavior, their segmentation will suffer.

Step 2: Identify Distinct Segments of Customers with Similar Purchase Behaviors

Step 2 involves analyzing a quantitative survey asking customers about their needs, attitudes, behaviors, and demographic characteristics. Standard statistical techniques can be used to determine the appropriate sample size and mix of potential customers. For the hypothetical overnight delivery example, the sample might include a mix of companies across the following dimensions:

- size—large, medium, small, home office
- industry—industrial, high technology, retail, etc.
- number of locations—many, few, one
- geographic coverage—domestic, multinational, global
- customer status—current customers, noncustomers

After the data has been collected, standard statistical techniques can be used to determine distinct segments of customers. Typically, a few variables will be responsible for highlighting the key differences between each segment. Segmentation of the overnight delivery market might result in four segments that primarily differ in terms of their complexity of needs (including multinational service), risk posture, and price sensitivity. Figure 5.2 (page 79) offers a simplified view.

Smaller companies with limited budgets may not have the resources to conduct the type of research described in Step 2. But that is not a good excuse for skipping the whole process of segmenting the market and selecting target customers. If anything, smaller companies need to know their target customers even better than the big companies do because investments must be tightly focused. As a smaller company, your best approach is to:

- Conduct the Step 1 qualitative research as thoroughly as possible within the available resources.
- Leverage your insights from Step 1 with any publicly available data that you can find to develop hypotheses about how customers might segment.
- Develop segment profiles based on the qualitative data that you have.

Figure 5.2 **Segmentation Map—Overnight Delivery Example**

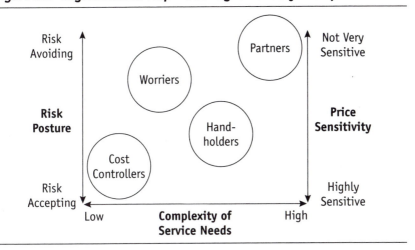

- Refine your segmentation, profiles, and target segments over time as you gain new insights about your customers.

Step 3: Create a Profile Describing Each Segment

The purpose of Step 3 is to describe each segment so we can create a mental picture of what the customers look like in each segment. A profile should give us a brief overview of each segment by highlighting its important characteristics. Components of a segment profile might include the following:

- primary needs
- size of the segment (Step 4 describes this process)
- purchase-decision maker (e.g., title/function within a company, head of household, primary shopper, etc.)
- decision-making criteria (how one service provider is selected over another)
- key attitudes—about your company, competitors
- usage and switching behavior—frequency and amount of usage, number of different service providers used
- demographic characteristics

Segment profiles are developed by analyzing the quantitative customer survey data, and selecting those variables that: (1) best describe each segment, and (2) are unique to each segment. Figure 5.3 on the following page shows a sample segmentation profile for the overnight delivery market (simplified for present purposes).

Step 4: Size Each Segment

A critical variable to examine prior to determining which segments to pursue is the size of each segment. It is important to look at segment size from four different perspectives:

1. The number of potential customers in each segment. What percent of the total population of potential customers falls into each segment? This number can be estimated from a quantitative survey by analyzing the percent of customers mapping to each segment, then projecting this on the total population. In the absence of quantitative research, a marketer must find other variables that can form the basis for sizing each segment, typically demographic variables. The growth rate in each segment's population should also be considered.

2. The total dollars being spent in each segment. What is the annual revenue potential of each segment? This number is estimated by multiplying the average annual spending per customer in a segment by the total number of customers in that segment. In addition, whether certain segments are expected to increase or decrease their spending in the future (based on their stated intentions) should also be considered.

3. The total profits available in each segment. What is the profit potential of each segment, after taking into consideration price sensitivity and the cost to serve each segment? If there are differences in the cost to serve, the average size of a purchase, or the price sensitivity of different segments, then profit per customer will vary by segment (and therefore total profits available in the segment).

4. The potential revenues from new products and services in each segment. What is the propensity of each segment to purchase new services? A quantitative segmentation study can test the reactions to several high-potential new product and service concepts, and estimate the purchase intent for each concept. Beyond the revenue and profit potential of new products and services, this information can be used to understand which segments are more receptive initial targets for new things.

Figure 5.3 Segmentation Profile—Overnight Delivery Example

	Partners	Hand-Holders	Worriers	Cost Controllers
Description	Sophisticated logistics needs and extensive internal operations	Complex logistics needs but internal capabilities are limited	Basic needs, no room for error	Basic needs, switch based on price
Top Needs	• Logistics outsourcing • Worldwide network • Training	• Broad service offering • Convenient locations • 24-hour support	• Precise delivery times • Tracking capabilities • High reliability	• Manage costs
Demographics				
• Industries	• Transportation	• Manufacturing	• Legal	• Retail
• Employees	• Largest	• Large	• Varied	• Small
• Locations	• Worldwide	• Nationwide/ Worldwide	• Several	• Few/One
Purchase Criteria	• Technical capability • Range of offerings	• Responsiveness • Technical capability	• Reputation	• Price
Purchase Behavior	• Centralized decisions by Logistics	• Centralized decisions by Logistics	• Decentralized decisions, buyer varies	• Decentralized decisions by Purchasing
Attitude Toward Our Company	• Best view of the company	• Favorable view of the company	• Moderate perceptions of the company	• Worst view of the company
Other Characteristics				
• Risk Posture	• Avoid	• Moderate	• Avoid	• Accepting
• Complexity	• High	• Moderate	• Low	• Low
• Importance of Logistics	• High	• High	• Low	• Low

Service companies can make costly mistakes by not considering all four of these sizing variables. For example, some segments may contain many potential customers, but each customer spends relatively little. On the contrary, some segments may spend a lot on services, but remain extremely price sensitive. Some segments may be very costly to serve. Finally, some segments may appear small on the surface but offer great future potential because of their receptivity to new products and services. Figure 5.4 shows a simplified example of sizing the different segments of the overnight delivery market.

Figure 5.4 **Segment Sizing—Overnight Delivery Example**

	Partners	Hand-Holders	Worriers	Cost Controllers
Percent of All Companies	5%	25%	20%	50%
Average Annual Spending per Company	$100,000	$40,000	$50,000	$10,000
Estimated Total Market Size	$1.7 billion	$3.4 billion	$3.4 billion	$1.7 billion

Step 5: Select the Target Segments

After profiling and sizing each segment, we are in a position to select the most desirable segments to serve. Selecting target customer segments is a two-step approach:

1. Establish selection criteria. With a cross-functional management team, agree up front on the criteria that would make a customer segment more attractive to pursue. Typical criteria to consider include the following:

- Strategic Attractiveness—fit with overall business strategy. How well do these customers and their needs fit with our company direction and identity?
- Customer Attractiveness—characteristics of customers. How intense are their unmet needs? How frequently and how much do they purchase? How loyal are they? How price sensitive are they?
- Competitive Attractiveness—number and size of key competitors. Can we become a dominant player in the segment? Can we differentiate or insulate ourselves from competition?

- Financial Attractiveness—segment size (number of customers, revenue per customer and total revenue potential, profit per customer and total profit potential). Can we earn sufficient revenues and profits from the segment to make it worthwhile?
- Technical and Operational Attractiveness—ability to cost-effectively serve the needs of a segment. What capabilities are required to serve the segment? How well does this fit with our strengths? Can we leverage the same infrastructure over multiple segments?
- Future Growth Attractiveness—growth rate, trends, and receptivity to new things. Will the segment become more attractive or less attractive over time?

2. Apply the criteria, evaluate each segment, and select the "right" customer segments to pursue. After establishing the criteria, evaluate each segment against each criterion. Again, a cross-functional management team is often better equipped to perform this analysis than any one individual or functional area. In selecting which segments to pursue, service companies should also consider the following trade-offs regarding the decision to serve only one segment versus serve several segments:

- Is any one segment attractive enough and large enough that the company could focus solely on that segment alone and still achieve their goals? Will their resources be adequate to dominate multiple segments?
- If different segments of customers interact with one another during their service experience, will this interaction make sense to each of these customer segments? Will any customers feel out of place?
- Will the frontline employees be able to effectively serve the needs of each customer segment? Will the company have to recruit and train differently to effectively serve each segment?
- If the company needs to serve multiple segments, which combinations of segments lend themselves to economies of scale? Specifically, can the company leverage the same infrastructure in serving several segments? Can the company leverage their brand identity and communication methods across multiple segments, or will they need to create separate brand identities and use different communication tactics to reach each segment?

Figure 5.5 (page 84) shows a sample segment evaluation for the overnight delivery market.

Figure 5.5 Segment Evaluation—Overnight Delivery Example

	Partners	Hand-Holders	Worriers	Cost Controllers
Size	◑	●	●	◑
Growth	●	◕	◔	◕
Competitive Intensity	●	◔	◔	○
Gross Margins	◕	◔	◔	○
Fit with Capabilities	◔	◕	●	●
Overall	◕	◔	◔	○

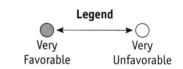

Legend

● ◄————————► ○
Very Favorable   Very Unfavorable

Step 6: Develop Approaches for Reaching Target Customers

Where most segmentation approaches fall short is that they do not provide an ability to efficiently identify and reach the target customers. After spending hundreds of thousands (and sometimes millions) of dollars, some service companies have found themselves with a slick-looking segmentation—interesting names given to the segments, a description, a psychographic profile, etc.—but have no idea how to find these customers. Their effort ends up being, for the most part, worthless. They can't organize to attract and serve these customers if they don't know who the customers are.

How do you find your target customers? A sound segmentation approach should be able to answer the following questions for each target segment:

- What do your customers read? What television programs do they watch?

- What trade shows do they attend and what associations do they belong to?
- What outlets do they typically purchase from?
- What methods of purchase do they prefer (e.g., phone, Internet, in person)?
- What other similar services and service providers do they use?
- What segment does each of your current customers belong to? Can you mark your customer database with the information?
- What mailing lists should you buy that would have a high occurrence of your target customers?

If these questions are built into the segmentation process up-front, then the target segments can be efficiently reached after being selected.

Dominating the Target Segments

Achieving the goal of dominating target customer segments requires developing segment-specific strategies—strategies that are all aligned against our target customers' needs and tightly integrated with one another. The first and most dominant marketing strategy that glues every other strategy together is the brand and positioning strategy. Chapter 6 discusses the topic of treating your brand like an asset. Once the brand strategy is created, the other core services marketing strategies must link with it. These strategies include the service offering strategy (Chapters 7–9), the service process strategy (Chapter 10), and the people strategy (Chapter 11).

How did Enterprise Rent-A-Car do it? They:

- uncovered an underserved segment of customers—those with cars being repaired
- branded their service to this target—their tag line says "We'll Pick You Up"
- tailored their offering—longer-term rentals, facilities located near repair shops
- addressed the needs of other interested parties—exclusive arrangements with insurance companies and auto repair shops
- aligned their process—pickup and delivery of cars for the customer
- hired the right kinds of people—those who develop strong relationships with auto repair shops

This integrated approach is powerful. While any one element might be copied, the entire approach is difficult to replicate with the same rigor and discipline.

Conclusion

Service market leaders dominate specific segments of customers. They want to be the top-of-mind provider and the first to be selected. They set goals to capture more than 50 percent of purchases make by their targeted customers. To these leaders, being number one with their target customers is more important than being the biggest player in an industry.

For many service companies, however, the lack of focus on target customers makes it difficult for them to meet the specific and unique needs of any particular segment of customers. Because services are intangible, customer expectations and the service delivery against those expectations are highly variable. The end result is an inability to differentiate from competition and generate superior profits. In contrast, service market leaders that attract the right customers can consistently deliver superior experiences and produce loyal, profitable customers.

A segmentation analysis and strategy is the way to determine who your target customers are. The process of segmenting service markets is best done following a six-step approach:

1. Identify different needs, attitudes, behaviors, and demographics across a variety of customers
2. Identify distinct segments of customers with similar purchase behavior
3. Create a profile describing each segment
4. Size each segment
5. Select the target segments
6. Develop approaches for reaching target customers

By avoiding the "all things to all customers" trap, service companies can deliver greater benefits and strip away unnecessary costs. Through this approach, successful service leaders emerge. They break away from their competition by consistently delivering greater value to their target customers. And it all starts with first selecting the right areas of focus and the right target customers.

CHAPTER 6

Treat Your Brand Like an Asset

SERVICE COMPANIES DELIVER AN INTANGIBLE experience to customers. For this reason, the brand identity is extremely important in helping customers understand the end benefits they will derive from the proposed service—both at the time they purchase it and after they have experienced it. Brand identity should be viewed as a long-term asset for the entire organization. To build a strong service brand, service companies must:

- Consistently invest in their brand to promote awareness and value perceptions in customers and prospects
- Implement their brand emphatically with hard-hitting positioning strategies that differ significantly from competitors. In fact, most powerful differentiation strategies are directly opposite of those from primary competitors
- Reinforce the brand asset, day to day, through all the marketing strategies of the organization
- Measure the brand asset over time and create specific strategies to carefully leverage its equity into new services and markets

Trying to understand what a brand is, let alone what it does or how to build one, has been one of the major marketing subjects discussed

Figure 6.1 **The Power of Strong Service Brands**

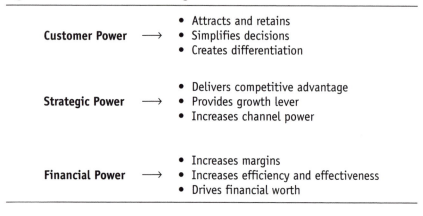

in the past decade. The challenge is further compounded when it concerns developing an intangible brand asset for an intangible service business that enables a label to be placed across a range of intangible experiences perceived by large numbers of independent customers. No wonder most people avoid the topic all together. Simply put, services are then highly prone to becoming perceived as commodities. Branding counteracts this natural pull from competitive markets. The power of a strong brand will positively impact a service business in the areas shown in Figure 6.1.

This chapter discusses a service company's brand as an asset and how to build this asset through brand strategies and positioning (later defined as *oppositioning*) strategies.

Branding the Service Experience

A brand is a powerful asset. Visionary and long-term oriented service companies build brands. However, customers and financial markets will watch closely to be sure that branding plans are not merely glorified ad campaigns in disguise. They will need to see that the messages to the market contained in the brand identity are, in fact, being delivered upon and that appropriate investments are being made.

Let's look at one of the most powerful service brands today—Starbucks. What comes to mind when you see their brand?

If you thought coffee beans, then you have missed the crux of their service brand. However, if you are like most coffee drinkers, you probably thought of the enjoyable experience of sipping great coffee in a pleasant atmosphere. The key factor in the brand identity for Starbucks is the experience—not the bag of beans or the cup of coffee. Starbucks has taken one of the oldest commodities in existence, coffee, and transformed it into a differentiated, global service enterprise. The management team at Starbucks has been brilliant in building their brand asset to such an extent that many people not only go out of their way to get a Starbucks grande skim latte with cinnamon, but pay an outrageous amount for it as well.

The roots of the Starbucks company provide the best insights into their brand strategy. Howard Schultz, its CEO, started Starbucks in Seattle's Pike Street market after traveling to Italy and seeing how their coffee parlors were such an integral part of the culture. Coffee drinking there was more of a social and self-indulging experience than it was in the United States' fast, convenience-oriented culture of the 1990s. Schultz rightly focused on creating the environment that would produce the experience of an Italian coffee parlor. He built coffee shops. Tangible elements such as high-quality coffee beans, good equipment, and trained coffee-making experts were a secondary focus in producing the service experience. Schultz rightly built the Starbucks brand to personify the experience.

Today, the vision for the Starbucks' brand might be summarized in the following statement:

> *Around the world, Starbucks will be the first stop for coffee drinkers seeking to experience the highest-quality fresh brewed coffee; Starbucks will be available everywhere and always fresh while maintaining a dedication to customer service and a premium service experience.*

The mix of tangible and experiential factors that help create the Starbucks brand are identified in Figure 6.2 (page 90). A service brand is built properly when both of these elements are at work.

Extending the Starbucks brand into new channels that do not employ all of the previously mentioned elements—such as allowing United Airlines to place the Starbucks brand on the coffee it serves—suggest trouble "brewing" for the brand. Starbucks cannot control the

Figure 6.2 **Starbucks Brand Characteristics**

TANGIBLE	EXPERIENTIAL
Highest-quality, best-tasting coffee Highest level of service Best selection Most convenient locations	Where you can provide yourself a little sef-indulgence every day Where you can meet friends and relax in a social atmosphere Where you can get coffee in a trendy atmosphere

coffee drinking experience on a United flight, because it doesn't control the equipment, the people making the coffee, the temperature at which the coffee is served, the in-flight atmosphere, and the bumpy ride caused by air turbulence. However, the United passenger receiving a cup with the Starbucks logo on it instantly becomes a Starbucks customer with the expectation that this coffee drinking experience will be like visiting a Starbucks outlet. Why? Because of Starbucks's great service execution and brand-building efforts. But the airline experience cannot possibly match up to that of the Starbucks coffee parlor.

Service companies cannot, therefore, merely sell their tangible elements (great coffee beans, in the case of Starbucks) under their service brand names without risking significant loss of equity in the brand. To market a new service or enter a new channel under an existing brand, the other elements that create the full experience and establish trust in the performance of the intangible service must be at work. Otherwise, a different brand name should be developed and promoted.

Finally, service brands have the special challenge of needing to convey trust. Brands are intended to convey the beliefs, values, and benefits of an intangible service and of the company producing the service. However, for service brands to be credible, they must establish trust with customers by promising only what can be consistently delivered. Many service companies use the faces and personalities of their leaders to build trust. This is why we see the CEOs of Southwest Airlines, Charles Schwab & Co., and Wendy's featured in their respective company's commercials.

Building Strong Service Brands

In an emerging industry, building a brand can be done relatively quickly and inexpensively. Without significant competitive "noise," industry pioneers have a unique brand-building opportunity—as exemplified by Netscape and Yahoo! in the Internet industry. Both joined the ranks of the top 100 brands worldwide within their first five years. They were able to do so, in large part, by initially giving away their service so that each became the default choice among Internet customers. While brands such as McDonald's and Pepsi spend hundreds of millions of dollars annually to maintain their brand equity in mature markets, these Internet companies spent only tens of millions of dollars to build theirs.

Most service industries can be classified as evolving. In these industries, the branding challenge is different. They must first discard their past "baggage"—having typically branded at the service-offering and tangible-attributes level (i.e., what the company offers). Instead, they need to focus on branding at the emotional level of customer experiences (i.e., how customers benefit from doing business with the company).

For example, in the health care industry, HMOs are struggling to build their brand identities. To do so, they must first break free of their popular image as bean-counting bureaucracies that put profits ahead of patients. This is no easy task. To build better brands, HMOs need to focus their brand-building strategies at the emotional level—their target customers' beliefs and values—and not at the tangible-product and service-attributes level. Several now portray themselves as "warm-hearted care-givers." For example, Aetna US Healthcare has been running television ads filled with customer testimonials. A teenage boy treated for a brain tumor looks into the camera and says, "I can tell you about gratitude." A liver-transplant patient attests, "I can tell you about regaining hope." Aetna and other HMOs want customers to *feel* that with their service, the patent's fate will be in the hands of doctors and not insurance administrators. This emotional branding level will provide a strong appeal for both customers and employees as well as provide a large enough umbrella to cover future service lines and channels.

Figure 6.3 Developing a Strong Service Brand

Step 1 Define Current Brand Images and Desired Brand Vision	Step 2 Develop the Positioning Strategy	Step 3 Implement the Brand Throughout the Organization
• For each target market, determine current brand image among customers and prospects.	• Develop and test positioning alternatives.	• Outline the internal and external requirements for fulfilling the brand vision.
• Determine the current brand images of competitors for each target market.	• Determine how the company will be known to customers in the future.	• Develop an internal and external communications plan.
• Define the company's desired future brand goals as they support the growth strategies.	• Finalize the strategies based on the value, uniqueness, credibility, and fit, including functional and emotional benefits, that the brand conveys.	• Develop functional strategies for implementing the brand.
• Create a vision of where the company would like to take it's brand.	• Determine the guidelines for using the brand with channels, other brands, etc.	• Develop metrics and a process for ongoing measurement of brand-building efforts.

Building a brand may appear to be more art than science. After all, isn't it just some creative types coming up with a good ad campaign or slogan? This is certainly *not* the case with successful service companies. Making your brand an asset requires as much strategy, focus, and execution as does creating new services or opening up new channels. The three steps to building strong service brands are outlined in Figure 6.3. Step 2, developing the positioning strategy, is the crucial strategy for creating a "be different" company. That strategy will be discussed next.

Promising Unique Benefits—the Positioning Strategy

A service company's brand provides an overall emotional identity that customers and employees can describe and identify with. It highlights the experience being promised by a company. For example, the Disney brand conveys a type of trusted entertainment experience that is for the family and involves activities such as rides, arcade games, kids' shows, and the like. It is one of the strongest brands on the planet. However, there are certainly lots of other theme parks and shows that would appear to be identical to Disney's offerings. So what is Disney's *unique* value being perceived by customers? And how does a service company take action to become perceived as unique by customers?

Customers perceive Disney Theme Parks to be the premium quality, full-scale, best people, most reliable experience, best activities, and the best value theme park compared to other parks. In building these perceptions over the years, Disney has made strategic promises to customers that it will provide the benefits customers want in a different way than competitors. Sometimes the actual benefit being provided—e.g., employees who act like entertainers—is different. Sometimes the way the benefit is delivered—e.g., impeccably clean facilities—is different. The point is that a service company needs to decide what specific, unique strategic promise it will make and deliver to its target customers. For product companies, this is usually referred to as their *positioning* and comes from the notion of placing and positioning tangible products next to their competitors on a shelf at a grocery store. For service companies, it is a promise of an intangible experience vis-à-vis competitors.

Whereas a brand is designed to last 10 to 100 years, the positioning strategy or promise usually has a 3 to 5 year life span. The positioning strategies represent the foundational bricks that build the overall brand image through the years. In addition, the positioning strategy is the core marketing strategy from which all other marketing strategies are derived.

A New Approach—Oppositioning

The acts of promise-making and promise-accepting run deep in American culture. People have natural hope in what the future may hold. But what causes a person to react to some promises more intensely than others? The answer to this question is how service companies need to establish their strategic promises. The following examples will illustrate a new principle of differentiation—*oppositioning*.

In 1963, Dr. Martin Luther King, Jr., gave a speech that promised a future where all men and women, regardless of color, would accept one another. While this promise did strike at the fundamental religious values deeply held by most Americans, that was not the primary reason for its profound impact. Rather, Dr. King's message was very different, or countercultural, to the events of the early 1960s. It was opposite to what was actually happening. Similarly, Israel and Palestine signed an agreement in 1995 declaring the promise of future peace. Beyond the fundamental value of peace that both sides wanted, this promise was so remarkable because it was a different, opposite outcome than most people believed possible at the time. And what if a six-year-old child promised to be responsible for the feeding of a new dog, would the parent react intensely to this promise? Probably not, because "that's what they all say." But the parent *would* react if the child promised to let the parent feed the dog while the child provided all the love. How counterintuitive! A different promise, one that runs opposite to what others are saying, garners the most impact.

The same holds true for the strategic promise of service companies. Customers buy intangible services with the hope of realizing the benefits promised by the provider. The fact is, however, that customers select providers based on the unique or different strategic benefits being promised by one provider vis-à-vis another. Said another way, a service provider's organizational promise to its customers is its main source of strategic differentiation. This promise will have greater impact the more it is different from, or opposite to, its competitors' promises. This is called oppositioning.

In the late 1970s, the major television networks were trying to capture the loyalty of avid sports fans (generally thought to be a large, homogeneous viewer group) by out-bidding one another for the rights to showcase events such as the Super Bowl, the World Series, and Wimbledon. Each network's "full-programming" strategic promise was similar to the promise of other networks. While it was certainly valued by customers, it was not distinguishable. Enter ESPN in 1979 with an oppositioning strategy. It became the first total sports network opposite a tide of full-programming networks. Today, it reaches 62 million homes as one of the highest-rated cable stations. With its launch of ESPN2, a twenty-four-hour sports channel, ESPN continues to differentiate itself by defining a unique promise within modern sports programming and broadcasting. And they are fulfilling it.

Another successful oppositioning strategy was executed during the 1980s when the downhill ski resort industry in the Rocky Mountains experienced a shakeout. The small, family-owned resorts in the region were going out of business due to intense competition from the larger resorts. Since all resorts offered the same basic promise ("Come one, come all, to a relaxing, enjoyable day of skiing"), the big resorts could promote and fulfill this promise better by simply spending more. If you were an owner of one of those near-extinct small resorts, what would you do? That's right, devise an oppositioning strategy— which is what the owners of Crested Butte did. Essentially, they promised customers that "You will find the roughest, toughest terrain at Crested Butte. In fact, only the most expert of skiers will find it enjoyable. Don't expect the glitzy atmosphere of Vail or Aspen. Come to our Western ski town for its expert skiing." And with this unique promise, Crested Butte thrives today. It was recently named one of the top resorts in North America by *Ski Magazine.*

Finally, oppositioning may not mean just being opposite to a direct competitor. It may mean thinking of the target customers and developing opposite alternatives to fulfill their core needs. An example from the airline industry will show how this works. Contrary to general opinion, the oppositioning strategy that launched Southwest Airlines was opposite car travel, not opposite big, full-service airlines. Southwest's management team did not begin by saying "If American and United are big and full-service, then, to be positioned uniquely, we should be a small, no-frills service." Instead, they innovated a *new,* more timely, safer way for people to travel to small cities (and for a reasonable price) than driving a car. Only in recent years has Southwest even considered other major airlines as direct competitors.

The Fundamentals of Oppositioning

There are three fundamentals of oppositioning strategy for service organizations. All three need to be a part of the oppositioning strategy.

1. An oppositioning strategy needs to define the strategic promise in terms of the *what*, the *how*, and the *who*. It should contain a definition of what the strategic benefit is to customers, a description of how the service experience will be realized by customers, and a commitment as to the people who will create and deliver the benefits to customers.
2. It must represent the entire company or business unit, not one particular service.
3. It must consider the need to "opposition" relative to customers who may consider performing the service themselves.

Deliver the *What*, the *How*, and the *Who*

IRI (Information Resources Inc.) is an information and research company competing fiercely with Nielson in the consumer products data collection and reporting industry. Over the years, IRI has clearly been the innovation leader but not necessarily the market leader. Why? Because they were not using their most powerful and unique strengths to compete. By adding the *how* and *who* elements, IRI created the desired oppositioning strategy. Figure 6.4 highlights how these elements provide the basis for IRI to grow for years to come.

Unfortunately, too many service organizations view the *how* and *who* elements as tactics rather than additional areas to innovate their

Figure 6.4 **IRI's Oppositioning Strategy**

The *What*	Develop leadership and technological innovations in the application of retail information for competitive advantage
The *How*	Create processes for and focus resources on helping client to more fully utilize the information and related technology being purchased
The *Who*	Form closer, longer-term business partnerships in which there are close relationships between peers at all levels

benefit promise to their customers. This is fine for product companies but leaves customers still searching for unique points of differentiation in the service world.

For a different example, suppose a leading fitness company employed the world's greatest fitness minds and experts. What would happen if its latest techniques and approaches to enable people to become physically fit was provided only in the form of tangible videos? Customers simply viewing videos would probably not realize the full promise potential of this fitness company. In essence, the fitness company would be oppositioning only on the *what*, and, moreover, only on one product. To truly leverage and grow the business, management should go in one of two directions:

1. Compete more as a fitness *product company* by competing not only on the *what* but also packaging the expertise into many product forms including videos, fitness equipment, clothing, or other tangible products to be sold through distribution. With this approach, the fitness company should regularly and systematically introduce new benefits and products slightly ahead of its customer's ability to use them and slightly ahead of competitors. This approach will give competitors a great deal of pause as they try to keep up using a "fast follower" strategy. Thus, the implementation of this oppositioning strategy is to continue developing innovative new concepts, uniquely packaging them, and then distributing selectively.

2. Compete more as a fitness *service company* that pursues market leadership beyond just the *what*—the leading-edge fitness expertise. This innovation paradigm reflects the desire to be the leader on *how* people should adapt and use the expertise, and focus on *who* will be involved with customers during the service experience. Example innovations for this service company are depicted in Figure 6.5 (page 98).

   For the fitness service company, the implementation of the oppositioning strategy would be to continue developing innovative new concepts as well as innovate new ways customers can have a unique service experience and new interactions with the "fitness doctors."

Figure 6.5 **A Fitness Service Company**

		Examples
The *What*	Leading-edge techniques	• In-water exercises
		• Working full muscle groups
The *How*	Accessible in company-owned fitness centers	• Atmosphere-controlled, small workout rooms
		• Individualized equipment
The *Who*	Containing breakthrough approaches in trainer-pupil interactions	• "Fitness doctors"—physical and behavioral therapists
		• Partnership workouts

From the two options discussed, which would you choose? Both can lead to success. The first alternative could enable the fitness company to be one of the leaders in the industry. The second alternative has the potential to make the fitness company the undisputed leader in the industry. And to the victor belongs the spoils.

Represent the Entire Organization

The second fundamental for oppositioning is that it must represent the entire organization or business unit, not just a particular service or product. For example, Charles Schwab's oppositioning strategy is to provide individual investors with a unique blend of benefits that include research—similar to full-service brokerage firms—as well as low trading prices—similar to discount brokerage firms. While individual services are given names to better identify and describe their individual features and benefits, the whole company is positioned opposite competitors. This is also what McDonald's does by "Mc-ing" so many food items. The McDonald's brand name is so strong and is such a primary determinant of customers' perceptions, that it can carry other products and services. It also works for McDonald's because, whether intentional or not, it has drifted more to the product side of the service-product continuum, where pursuing a traditional product-brand management approach (which focuses on the positioning of the Big Mac versus the Whopper of Burger King) is appropriate.

"Opposition" Against Your Customers

The third fundamental for oppositioning is dealing with the fact that for many service companies, their customers are their biggest competitor. For example, many large corporations have established their own internal management consulting groups to replace or supplement the work of outside consultants.

Service often means doing for customers what they can't do for themselves. A mind-set needs to permeate the service organization to innovate more continuously because the "in-house" competitor (i.e., the customer) will learn and grow the skills necessary to eventually perform the provided service themselves. This phenomenon is especially a threat to continuation of revenues if the service being provided becomes a high-cost item and becomes perceived as a commodity that can easily be done internally. So how do you opposition against your customers? Simply do only the things your customers have strategically decided is not their core business or for which they do not have core competencies. Being opposite customers' skills leads to strong customer partnerships and integration between service provider and service customer.

Permeating the Business Enterprise

The oppositioning strategy must be fully supported by every functional area of the business. Otherwise, customers will not feel the difference. The promise will appear empty to customers—like an advertising gimmick.

The video rental service industry serves as an example. Throughout much of the 1990s, it has been led and dominated by the innovativeness of Blockbuster Entertainment. To be able to grow and prosper in this industry, service competitors need to have oppositioning strategies. Hollywood Video is attempting to do just that. Hollywood Video wants to portray Blockbuster's service environment, essentially the *how* and the *who*, as generic and for the masses. In contrast, Hollywood Video wants to stand for the excitement and the imagery of the motion picture industry. A Hollywood Video store environment is described as "vibrant, sexy, appealing to the MTV generation." There are walls of televisions, rock music, bright lights, and a neon decor. Clerks wear tuxedo shirts and bright red bow ties. So what of the results? In recent years, Hollywood Video has generated a higher per-store volume than Blockbuster. What do you suppose would happen if Hollywood Video also innovated the *what* and offered something other than videocassette movie rentals? For example, in keeping with the fun and interactive theme of the organization, why not have this happen at home? Hollywood Video could promote "home movie parties" that center around selected videos with interludes spliced into the film at interesting junctures. "What will the main character do next?" or "guess the ending?" type of questions could be asked, which would allow party-goers to interact with one another. This type of *what* innovation might change the way we think about renting movies for home entertainment.

But what of Blockbuster Entertainment? Its current thrust seems to be to grow by diversifying beyond the videocassette rental business into a national array of differentiated entertainment offerings. These include Block Party, an adults-only arcade and amusement center where "grownups go to kid around"; Blockbuster Golf & Games, golf facilities designed for families; and Discovery Zone, which offers an enormous play arena for children from ages three to twelve. Blockbuster has even issued its own Visa card for discounts at all entertainment venues. Hopefully, as part of its growth strategy, management will continue inventing new value in their core video rental business. Chapter 8 describes one such strategy being pursued by Blockbuster.

Developing an Oppositioning Strategy

Developing an oppositioning strategy requires service companies to simultaneously grasp a number of marketing concepts to form a solid foundation. Although these marketing concepts are broadly applicable to any company, there are specific applications unique to service companies: the concept of brand management and the concept of organization.

Oppositioning and Brand Management

Service companies like Promus Hotels, more so than product companies like Procter & Gamble, need to build the overall corporate brand
name ahead of, or at least equal to, the brand names of individual service lines. For Promus, its individual service line is its hotel chain
Embassy Suites. Having grasped this concept, FedEx puts its name on
everything from FedEx software to FedEx tracking. They have solid
rationale for this principle: services are intangible and, therefore, gain
considerable benefit from the trust and credibility reassurance that a
good brand name can deliver.

In addition, most sizable service leaders compete (find their points of
innovation) on the integration of their independent service lines.
Another example of the power of a corporate brand name is GE Capital,
who promotes the GE Capital name for all its service lines. GE Capital
attracts and retains sophisticated customers because it can handle both
the unusual, highly customized leasing deals as well as the standard leasing programs. If your company needs a standard corporate auto-leasing
program, GE Capital can do it. But if your company needs variances
because of international restrictions or because your human resources
department wants a special buyout provision as a perk for executives,
you would definitely want GE Capital. They can bring the necessary
expertise to your situation easily and with high-quality results.

If a service company only promotes the brand names of specific
service lines and not the overall company, then it portrays itself as
more of a product company that offers standard products to homogeneous markets. If the homogeneous markets are defined very narrowly, then this branding approach will probably be quite workable.
Otherwise, the company will forever be stuck in a nondifferentiated,
commodity marketplace where customers expect this branded product to be of increasingly higher quality and decreasingly lower price.

Oppositioning and Organization Credibility

Another key oppositioning marketing concept concerns the credibility gap (or the over-promised gap). This gap is the distance between
what is promised (and therefore expected) and what is perceived to

actually have been delivered. The challenge? This perception varies by person. With products, one can compare their performance against a set of predefined standards. With products, there can be a breakdown in sales, distribution, customer service, etc., but if the product still performs, the positioning promise is upheld. Not so with services. With services, the *whole* organization must be behind the promise or the company can't deliver on it. Inconsistent delivery hurts organizational credibility, and trust is broken.

Conclusion

The oppositioning strategy can be developed only with information and feedback from the marketplace. Any other approach is only an academic exercise. While it may produce some breakthrough strategy ideas, no single strategy will be implemented.

To make oppositioning work, an organization cannot be focused exclusively on market share. IRI needed to be willing to relinquish market share in the form of number of customers in order to grow revenues with a focus on revenues per customer. The goal should be 80 percent-plus customer share, as nontargeted customers should be shed once a minimum economy of scale level is reached (and because of technology, these thresholds continue to decline for most service industries). If accomplished, this leads to higher margins for a service company. In fact, one could argue that when a company reaches 50 percent overall market share, it is time to find profitable niches that would result in a 25 to 30 percent overall market share within the industry. In short, the goal should be to always find opposite niches to dominate. This is hard for the ego that wants to be *big*—but good for the ego that wants to be a *profitable* market leader.

PART III

Creating Unique, Valued Services

CHAPTER 7

Innovate Continuously

CCC INFORMATION SERVICES, A NETWORK SER-
vices company in the insurance industry, has grown its revenues from
$30 million in the early 1990s to $160 million in 1997. It prides itself
on being an organization obsessed with creating value and inventing
new benefits for customers. And CCC perceives its role as that of an
industry leader, shaping the industry's evolution. Management measures the degree of value created by finding out what customers think.
They gauge the company's effectiveness in execution by doing things
faster than and differently from their competitors.

CCC's management team spends much of their time and energy
on growing the company through innovation. What sets CCC apart is
their unwavering commitment to a set of market-driven fundamentals for continuously innovating a service business:

- continuously challenging the uniqueness of the benefits being
  offered to customers—belief in the need to change the basis of
  competition
- maintaining an entrepreneurial spirit—no matter how big they
  become
- encouraging risk-taking by employees

- pursuing close relationships with customers rather than keeping them at arm's length
- creating a portfolio of new offerings on a continual basis that customers value

CCC is convinced that winning does not come from bigness, operational leadership, and high quality. CCC has always believed in invention and timing. And to win at this game an organization has to be focused, first and foremost, on customers in order to understand and create solutions to customers' needs before competitors do. Being the industry innovator is a mind-set or philosophy at CCC. This mind-set is implemented through strategies that: balance predictability and risk taking; attract people who are the best of the best in the industry; and offer a team-structured environment where talented people can thrive and feel a sense of autonomy.

Continuous innovation does not just happen. It requires up-front strategy, planning, and preparation, as well as ongoing resource commitment, effective processes, and management support. This chapter outlines a framework that service companies can use to create continuous innovation in their organizations.

Continuous Service Innovation

Who was the first company to offer travel reservation capabilities over the Internet? The first bank to offer ATMs? The first airline with a frequent flier program? The first telephone company to offer voice-mail services or caller ID? The first fast-food company to bundle together meal items and form a value meal? The first credit card company to offer free car rental insurance if charged on the credit card? Who knows—who cares? These services are now widely available from most companies in their respective industries. Today, they are "tickets to entry," with customers expecting and practically demanding them.

Across most service industries, the following five characteristics hold true:

1. Service markets evolve and mature more rapidly than do product markets.

2. Competitors quickly and easily copy new service introductions.
3. Competitors hold clearly defined market positions that they "own" and from which they are difficult to dislodge.
4. Service market boundaries are "soft" and fluid. Niches combine and break apart on an ongoing basis.
5. "Be better" strategies ultimately fade as differentiators. Service improvement efforts such as raising quality, reengineering for cost efficiency, and standardization offer a diminishing positive benefit.

As a result, service life cycles are short. Services are often difficult to patent, have low barriers to entry (e.g, require small capital investment), and frequently depend on the expertise of individual employees who can easily move from company to company. Consequently, competitors quickly enter the market with similar offerings. Today's unique service becomes tomorrow's commodity service where customers can't tell the difference. Service market "truths" predict this phenomenon.

Historical research on new product and service development says, as expected, that success rates are always below 100 percent—except for companies that choose not to launch any new services. In reality, the best innovators achieve no better than an 80 percent success rate with new service launches, with the average success rate for all service companies being closer to 60 percent (Griffin 1997). This number is even lower for breakthrough new services that attempt to change the nature of competition.

How does a service company deal with these two conflicting challenges: the need to innovate continuously and the certainty (and even desirability) of launching new service failures? Successful service innovators create a portfolio of offerings that align with their risk tolerance (see Figure 7.1, page 108).

That is, they constantly develop and launch new services intended to address customers' most intense and pervasive needs. Successful innovators create a portfolio of offerings to diversify risk and provide a balanced investment approach to innovation. Risk is measured in two dimensions: newness to the market and newness to the company. Clearly, services that are new to the market and require capabilities that are new to the company represent the most significant risk. They also tend to offer the greatest returns.

Figure 7.1 **Portfolio Approach to Service Innovation**

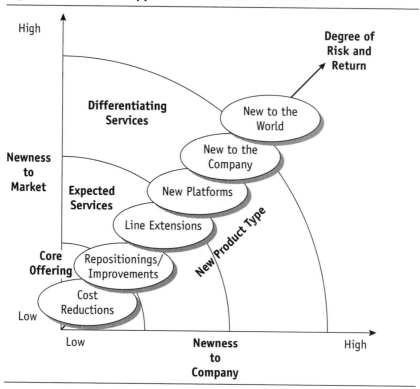

In summary, two things are crucial for growing service companies: continuous innovation and a balanced portfolio of new services. Making these two things happen concurrently can be tremendously difficult. The starting point is the development of an innovation strategy. In conjunction with such an innovation strategy, successful innovators also apply the following practices:

- Use of a systematic new service development process (see Chapter 12)
- Use of multifunctional teams with dedicated team members
- Commitment and appropriate involvement of top management
- Adequate resource allocation
- Compensation and rewards that stimulate an entrepreneurial environment
- Measurement of return on innovation efforts

Developing an Innovation Strategy

Innovation does not just happen. And a portfolio of high-potential new service concepts does not come from conducting a few half-day brainstorming meetings. Continuous innovation starts with a proactive plan—an innovation strategy—for how the company's goals will be achieved through innovation. In many service companies, business strategy and innovation efforts are not aligned. Investments in new service development may or may not result in helping achieve business objectives. The role of an innovation strategy is to formally align innovation efforts and business strategy. An innovation strategy enables a company to answer "Yes" to the question: "If we invest in new service development, will we be happy with where those efforts take us?"

The problem in many service companies is that innovation efforts can easily get off track—or never get on the right track. Time and again, service companies fall into several common innovation pitfalls:

• Lack of strategic alignment. Teams are working on new service projects that are not linked to the company's strategy and goals. These projects sounded like good ideas at one time, but now they are out of scope. Eventually they get killed or die a slow death. Team members become frustrated and feel like their time has been wasted.

• Underallocation of resources. Many service companies set aggressive goals for innovation but dedicate only a handful of people to the effort. One networking company we encountered established a five-year goal of $2 billion in incremental revenue from new services. Can you guess how many people they dedicated to achieving that goal? Two! The outcome can be easily predicted.

• Fragmentation of resources. Some companies refuse to kill projects. They delay difficult decisions, and projects meander on too long. As a result, the company's resources are stretched too thinly across too many projects, and no project receives the attention it needs. Management and team members both become frustrated when nothing gets to market. The root cause is the inability to say "No" to certain projects. Successful innovators focus on a limited number of high-priority projects.

• Lack of breakthrough innovation. Some service companies focus all their innovation efforts on low-risk, minor service improvements.

They don't develop services that are truly new and different. Often, the root causes are incentives and career paths that don't encourage risk taking, short planning horizons (e.g., must have results in ninety days), and leadership styles that do not accept (let alone reward) failures.

One financial services company had not created a breakthrough innovation in fifteen years. Nine out of ten people in the company had never seen their company develop a breakthrough new service. Employees did not know what one looked or felt like. Several problems contributed to this lack of breakthrough innovation: the incentive system was focused exclusively on operational efficiency; team members from failed new service efforts were marked for life, their careers permanently damaged; and frequent job movement in the marketing department encouraged managers there to focus on projects that could be completed within eighteen months. Under such circumstances, breakthrough innovation could never occur.

• No pre-defined criteria for success. In an attempt to be entrepreneurial, some companies do not consistently define and apply hurdles to all new service projects. "Bring me your ideas, and I'll know a successful one when I see it" is the phrase heard from all too many senior managers. In actuality, this attitude has a demoralizing impact on new service development teams. Without predefined goals and targets, teams get insufficient guidance. How can they hit an undefined, moving target? Go/no-go decisions are perceived to be (and often are) based on the unpredictable "gut feel" of a few senior managers.

An innovation strategy (Kuczmarski 1997) helps prevent many of these common pitfalls. It provides an overall description of the role that new services will play in satisfying the growth goals of the company. Specifically, an innovation strategy contains these three components:

1. The new service growth gap is the financial expectations for new service revenues and profits, typically over a five-year period. The growth gap chart outlined in Chapter 3 requires additional details to highlight the portion of the overall company growth goals expected to come from new services.
2. New service vision and strategic roles are the scope boundaries for new services and the strategic objectives new services should serve in supporting the business strategy.

3. Screening criteria are the filters that help determine which new services are most attractive to pursue to yield success.

For an effective innovation strategy, these three components need to be integrated and consistent. For example, if the new service growth goals are aggressive, then the vision and strategic roles must support a higher-risk portfolio of new services, and the screening criteria must establish aggressive hurdles to be met.

New Service Growth Gap

The purpose of developing a new service growth gap is twofold:

1. Align management's expectations regarding the planned financial contribution from new services. Most companies' financial expectations initially vary, usually quite substantially, among senior managers. Until expectations are in sync, new service development efforts will inevitably suffer. Figure 7.2 illustrates a sample new service growth gap after consensus is reached across a broad range of senior managers.

Figure 7.2 **Five-Year New Service Growth Gap**

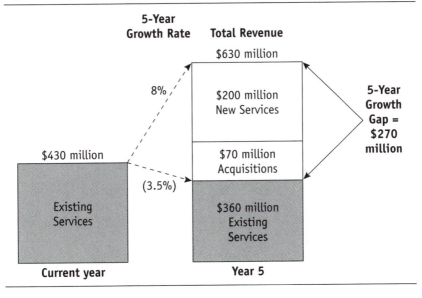

5-Year Growth Rate | Total Revenue

$630 million

8%

$200 million New Services

5-Year Growth Gap = $270 million

$430 million

$70 million Acquisitions

(3.5%)

Existing Services

$360 million Existing Services

Current year

Year 5

2. Identify the resources required to achieve these financial goals. A telecommunications supplier established a five-year goal of $300 million in incremental revenues from new services. However, in the previous five years, only three new services that achieved greater than $30 million in annual revenue were launched in this company's entire industry. Assuming a new service success rate of 60 percent and a balanced portfolio, this company would need to seriously ramp up its new service development activities—launching approximately thirty-four new services over the next five years (including fourteen expected failures). (See Figure 7.3.)

Figure 7.3 **Bottom-Up New Service Development Requirements (Telecommunications Company)**

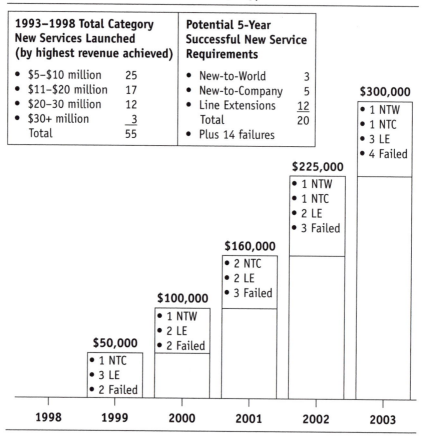

1993–1998 Total Category New Services Launched (by highest revenue achieved)		Potential 5-Year Successful New Service Requirements	
• $5–$10 million	25	• New-to-World	3
• $11–$20 million	17	• New-to-Company	5
• $20–30 million	12	• Line Extensions	12
• $30+ million	3	Total	20
Total	55	• Plus 14 failures	

$300,000
• 1 NTW
• 1 NTC
• 3 LE
• 4 Failed

$225,000
• 1 NTW
• 1 NTC
• 2 LE
• 3 Failed

$160,000
• 2 NTC
• 2 LE
• 3 Failed

$100,000
• 1 NTW
• 2 LE
• 2 Failed

$50,000
• 1 NTC
• 3 LE
• 2 Failed

| 1998 | 1999 | 2000 | 2001 | 2002 | 2003 |

In concert, they would have had to dramatically increase the resources dedicated to new service development to achieve such aggressive goals—more people, more capital spending, larger R&D and information technology budgets, more market research and test marketing, and more advertising and promotion. And, of course, more management time and attention.

Key inputs into the new service growth gap are perspectives from senior managers, historical new service performance of the company, historical new service performance of competitors, and company financial and strategic plans. The ultimate benefit from assimilating these inputs is an agreed-upon target and expectations for service innovation efforts. Companies with more aggressive growth gaps may need to define their new service vision more broadly than they currently do and establish strategic roles that encourage greater risk taking.

New Service Vision and Strategic Roles

Often a company's strategic plan does not provide enough guidance on the types of new services to be developed. As a result, service developers are often left guessing rather than having concrete answers to such key strategic questions as:

- What objective is the company trying to support with new services?
- What types of new services would fit the company's strategy, and what types would clearly be out of scope?
- To what degree should the new service portfolio help the company enter totally new areas as opposed to defending current businesses?
- What level of risk is the company willing to accept with its new service portfolio?
- How expansive should the new service portfolio be?

The new service vision and strategic roles provide a framework to ensure that new services developed will fit the company strategy.

A new service vision is a concise, future-oriented statement that defines the industry where the company will compete and its desired position within that industry. The three components of a new service vision are:

1. Define the market where the company competes (or wants to compete)—e.g., the scope boundaries defining and identifying which market (or parts of a market) should be targeted for new service development and which areas are out of scope. The more aggressive a company's growth goals, the more broadly they may need to define their market scope.
2. Define the company's desired position in the industry. How would the company define its leadership role in the market? Does the company desire to be the most profitable? The dominant player in certain niches?
3. Define the range of benefits to be provided to customers—e.g., the benefits the company will focus on delivering to customers, consistent with its brand and positioning strategy. Will the company focus on reducing delivery time or customer wait time? Improving personalized service? Applying technology to improve ease of use for customers? Providing pervasive customer access? New service developers need some broad guidelines for the types of benefits they should focus on delivering.

Figure 7.4 (page 115) shows a sample new service vision for a residential telecommunications provider.

Strategic roles help identify more specific ways in which new services will support the business strategy. In particular, they define how the new services can help solidify and grow the current business, as well as propel the company into new areas. The key requirement is that all strategic roles must support a business objective.

New service strategic roles can be classified as either requisite or expansive. Requisite roles describe functions that new services can satisfy in defending, enhancing or increasing the competitiveness of existing services, within existing markets, for existing customers. Expansive roles help direct a company to develop services for going outside of the confines of the current business—into new markets, offering new benefits, applying new technologies, and targeting new customer segments.

For a given company, new service strategic roles tend to fulfill one or more of the following business requirements:

Figure 7.4 New Service Vision (Telecommunications Company)

We will be recognized as the leading communications solution provider for small businesses in our five-state market. Our products and services will assist small businesses in increasing their efficiency and competitiveness.

	Components
Focus Areas	• Delivery and management of integrated communication solutions (voice, data, and video) • Services to help retain existing small-business customers • Services to attract the emerging Small Office/Home Office (SOHO) market
Key Customer Benefits	• Reliability—fixing problems in a responsive manner • Customized solutions that meet company-specific needs • Unequaled post-sale service • Applications that solve business needs and make our customers more competitive
Sources of Competitive Advantage	• Long-term established customer relationships • Local business presence • Expertise of our people • Recognized and respected brand

1. Penetrate certain customer segments—defend existing segments or penetrate new segments
2. Deliver specific customer benefits—eliminate problems with current services, enhance existing benefits, or deliver entirely new benefits
3. Leverage or apply certain technologies and capabilities—leverage existing capabilities or incorporate new capabilities
4. Use certain distribution channels—enhance existing channels or enter new channels
5. Respond to competitive pressures—respond to or preempt a competitive entry
6. Leverage brand equities—enhance or extend brand equities

Figure 7.5 (page 116) outlines strategic roles for the previously mentioned telecommunications company.

Strategic roles help define and guide the desired portfolio mix of new services. New services that satisfy requisite roles are typically less risky—e.g., cost reductions, repositionings, improvements, and line extensions. New services that satisfy expansive roles are typically

Figure 7.5 **New Service Roles (Telecommunications Company)**

Requisite Roles	Expansive Roles
(ways that new services can defend and extend the *current* business)	(ways that new services can propel the company into *new* areas)
• Retain existing customers • Differentiate from competition on integration of services • Reduce cost of installation, maintenance, and customer support for current services • Deliver current services through a service bureau or outsourcing approach	• Expand into the Small Office/Home Office (SOHO) market • Expand into cities not currently served in the five-state geography • Expand into retail channels

more risky—e.g., new platforms, new-to-the-company services, and new-to-the-world services.

An electric utility trying to develop a more expansive portfolio of services mapped its current new service development projects against a newly defined set of strategic roles. They found out that 60 percent of the projects were fulfilling expansive roles; that seemed appropriate, given the company's aggressive growth goals. However, 80 percent of these expansive projects were aligned against only *one* role—the application of a new technology. Overall, the company's new service portfolio was too skewed in one direction and needed realignment.

Screening Criteria

Screening criteria are objective measures for evaluating the relative attractiveness of new service opportunities. Attached to each criteria are hurdles that a new service idea, concept, or prototype must exceed in order to move on to the next stage of development.

The purpose for developing and applying new service screening criteria is as follows:

1. Focus investments. Screening criteria help eliminate ideas that appear to not meet corporate hurdles. As a new service concept moves through the development process, the investment goes

up. Screening criteria help an organization avoid investing in the wrong projects.

2. More rapidly complete high-potential projects. By focusing new service development efforts on the highest-potential projects, companies can put more dedicated teams onto such projects to ensure timely completion.

3. Provide objective goals. Screening criteria provide objective measures that new service development teams can shoot for, mitigating the gut feel or champion-driven screening approach used by many companies. Two CEOs struck an agreement to develop and test-market a new energy management service. This service would enable homeowners to monitor their energy usage by appliance and by time of day and then to modify their usage behavior to save money. The initiative provided positive PR value for both companies. Customers, however, were not very interested. The benefits were not compelling enough to warrant using the product. Objective, market-driven measures were replaced with subjective, management-driven measures. The development team felt powerless to kill the project even after determining it would never achieve any reasonable financial hurdles. Both companies suffered financial losses, and eventually the test market was discontinued.

To receive the greatest benefit from developing and applying screening criteria, several key principles should be followed:

• Screening criteria should be agreed to in advance. This reduces the likelihood of surprises and midcourse changes. Nothing is more frustrating for a new service development team than when they think they have met the corporate hurdles but find out the hurdles have changed.

• Screening results should be presented to a cross-functional management team. All appropriate functional areas of the company should be represented in order to critically evaluate ideas and offer opinions as ideas move through the process. Too often, companies say "We don't need the environmental department involved until the end" or "Legal will just slow us down if we get them involved up front." In reality, if important issues get raised and addressed early in the process, the overall time-to-market can be reduced.

• Screening is not a one-time event. It should be performed at several points throughout the new service development process (see Figure 7.6, page 119), prior to ever committing to the next level of investment in a project. Screening also builds momentum for and provides education about a new service to the broader organization. If momentum is there and education occurs, fewer roadblocks crop up late in the process that might kill a good idea.

• The same categories of screens should be maintained throughout the process. Although the specific questions and hurdles may change, the categories of screening criteria should remain the same to ensure consistency. Typical screening categories are:

- Strategic fit
- Customer need intensity
- Market attractiveness
- Technical and operational feasibility
- Regulatory/Environmental/Legal Feasibility
- Financial attractiveness

• As a project moves through the process, the hurdles associated with each screening category should become more rigorous and the measures more quantifiable. Rigor should increase because the cost of failure goes up dramatically as ideas move into later stages of the process.

• Screening hurdles should vary by type of new service. New services with higher risk (e.g., new to the world, new to the company) may be allowed more development time, but must meet higher financial return hurdles. Similarly, new services with lower risk (e.g., line extensions, product improvements) may have lower financial requirements to get approved for launch.

Conclusion

Innovation is necessary for growing service companies. But service companies cannot sit back and hope one or two ideas will provide the needed boost. Instead, they need a sustained, continuous

Figure 7.6 **Screening Points in the New Service Development Process**

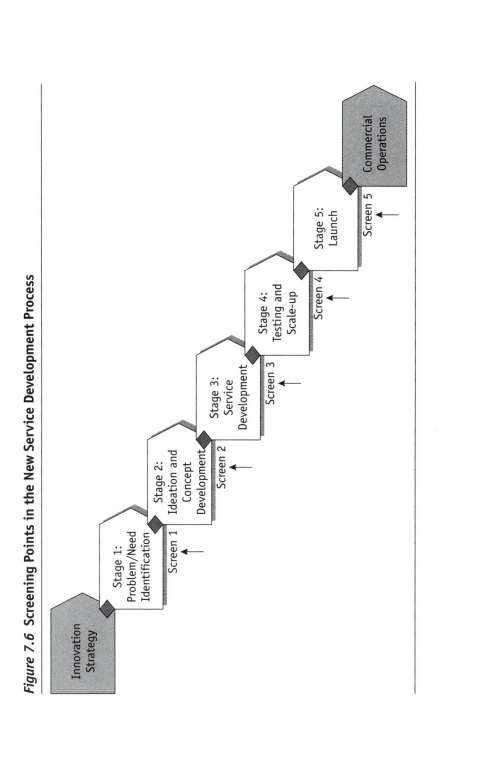

effort to achieve service innovation and create a balanced portfolio of new services closely linked to business objectives. Chapters 8 and 9 provide ideas and examples for how to re-innovate current service offerings and create totally new offerings. Chapter 12 outlines a process for continuous innovation.

CHAPTER 8

Revitalize Current Services

A FRIEND OF OURS LIVES IN A DENSELY POPU-
lated Chicago neighborhood where three video rental stores are
located within walking distance of his home. The closest is a West
Coast Video, only half a block away at the end of his street. Three
blocks south is an urban shopping mall with a new Hollywood Video
store. Blockbuster Video is farthest away, being about a ten-minute
walk from his home. With these multiple choices, how does a video
rental store get someone's attention? After all, aren't video rental
stores all the same? They all certainly seem to have the exact same
offering—the usual mix of new-release video rentals, shelves full of
older titles in every movie category imaginable, video game rentals,
and music.

Video rental stores were all pretty much the same until Blockbuster
made a bold move in 1998. Blockbuster began guaranteeing availability of people's favorite new release titles. How often do customers go
to the video store only to find that the new movie they want is out of
stock? Customers end up settling for a movie they didn't really want,
or maybe they leave without a movie at all, frustrated that the one
they wanted wasn't available. Blockbuster found a creative way
around this problem and has revitalized the core service offering

through a powerful new service guarantee. A lot of customers, including our friend, now make the extra effort to visit a Blockbuster video store.

How did Blockbuster do it? They started by renegotiating contracts with video distribution companies and studios and shifted to a revenue-sharing model rather than purchasing videos outright. Under the new model, Blockbuster pays substantially less for each videotape, then shares total video rental receipts with the distribution companies and studios. As a result, Blockbuster can now stock far more copies of hit titles because they pay far less for each title. More copies of the tapes are in stock as soon as a new release arrives in Blockbuster stores. Remember, Blockbuster now *guarantees* availability. If the movie is out of stock, customers get a raincheck to receive that movie rental free. In the three months of offering the new guarantee, Blockbuster's worldwide same-store video rentals increased over 13 percent from the prior year.

Blockbuster saw their core service offering—new-release video rentals—becoming more and more competitive. New companies entered the market, video rental stores began saturating every community, and prices started to fall. How could Blockbuster maintain favorable pricing in such a competitive environment? They revitalized the core service offering using a powerful technique called a *service guarantee*. This chapter will describe a variety of techniques for fending off price and margin erosion of current service offerings.

The Warning Signals of Tired Service Offerings

Services move through their life cycles more rapidly than do products. In general, services are more quickly and easily duplicated, resulting in parity offerings that are difficult to differentiate. Customers can't tell the difference, so they select a provider based on lowest price or availability.

Services generally get tired for one of three reasons:

1. Customers take the offering for granted because they perceive no difference between providers. By the time a service offering is mature, companies have flooded the market with comparable offer-

ings. Customers can't tell the difference. For example, although many people have an affinity for their independent insurance agent or financial planner, they will change insurance carriers in a heartbeat to secure a lower rate. Unless you have made a claim and experienced firsthand how a particular carrier responds, you probably perceive little, if any, difference between them. The result—frequent switching among insurance carriers.

2. Marketing efforts get boring and repetitive. In many service industries, customers hear the same messages and receive the same promotions over and over again. The fast-food chains have become notorious for promotional tie-ins with hit movies, primarily aimed at children. As new high-budget movies are launched, the fast-food chains are quick to lock in agreements with the studios releasing them. Games, action figures, collectible cups, and advertisements all play a part in these promotional efforts. Food sales get a quick boost from the promotion; then it ends and "business as usual" returns. Although these promotional efforts breathe temporary life into the business, they are unable to reinvigorate the core service offering in a lasting way.

3. People and systems delivering the service get complacent. Over time, service companies can begin to take their services, and their customers, for granted. The service delivery becomes routine and mechanical. Customers feel like they are just a number in the system. For years, local cable companies had a lock on their markets. Customers typically had no choices. As a result, customers had to put up with poor service, no scheduled appointments, and long wait times to get anything done. Cable companies became complacent in their monopoly position. Today, competing cable offerings from Regional Bell Operating Companies (RBOCs), other new cable entrants, and competing technologies such as satellite TV are stealing customers from cable companies. The monopoly advantage is over, and the traditional cable companies must reinvigorate their service delivery and offerings or risk losing much of their customer base.

Identifying tired services is not difficult. The most common warning signals are:

- Slowing/declining financial results: slow revenue and profit growth. The service has entered a mature phase where many competitors are fighting it out for their share of a slow-growing market.

- Increased price sensitivity: increased customer price sensitivity and inability to maintain price points. Customers are more educated and informed about their options and seek out lower-cost distribution channels or niche service providers that offer lower prices or greater perceived value.
- Increased customer switching/reduced loyalty: increased switching of customers between providers (e.g., lack of customer loyalty). Customers frequently switch among different providers based on price promotions, convenience, etc., rather than continuing to remain loyal to one company.
- Lack of perceived difference: inability of customers to distinguish among offerings from different companies. Customers cannot articulate any unique value offered by various providers.

If you see these telltale signs, then it's time to revitalize your service offerings—or eliminate some offerings altogether.

Revitalization Objectives

What, then, should be done with services at the end of their life cycles? The answer is to do something—not just agonize over the situation and do nothing. Revitalize service offerings that have potential. Eliminate offerings that don't offer growth, margin enhancement, or strategic advantage. Don't just let them die a slow death.

The objectives of revitalizing current service offerings can take one of four forms:

1. Reposition to expand the customer base. Companies can reposition on a new strategic benefit that helps reestablish growth in the core service offering by attracting new customer segments.
2. Extend offerings to increase revenues from or maintain current price levels with the current customer base. Companies can extend their offerings by increasing the value delivered.
3. Lock in customers (retain a greater percentage of current customers) by taking actions that increase loyalty.

4. Support commitments to deliver a full-line service offering to customers while improving profitability by curtailing investments.

Repositioning Offerings to Expand the Customer Base

Some offerings can be revitalized by modifying them—specifically, repositioning them—to attract new customers into the market. In some cases, companies may need to strip down premium services to make them appeal to a mass audience. In other cases, companies need to find ways to attract a younger or older generation of customers into the market for their services. Regardless, they must uncover new benefits desired by different segments of customers and then modify their services to deliver those benefits.

Two approaches to repositioning existing services to reach new customer segments are:

1. Create a new image for a service and deliver an important benefit desired by a particular customer segment not currently using the service.

Creating a new image and attracting a different customer segment are exactly what bowling is trying to do. For years, bowling was about run-down alleys, bad food, and tacky matching shirts. Today, the sport is cleaning up its act and introducing elements such as pulsating rock music, artificial fog, and glow-in-the-dark balls and pins, making it one of the hippest games in town.

Since the 1980s, participation in the sport has waned, league play has dropped considerably, and facilities have aged and fallen into disrepair. Hundreds of bowling alleys have called it quits.

Then came the glow. In the past four years, at least a third of the 6,800 bowling centers in the United States have revamped their facilities so they can offer glow bowling. . . . It's so popular, in fact, especially among teens and young adults, that the Palisades IV features four sessions every weekend. On Saturday nights, the 10 o'clock session runs for two and a half hours, then the house is cleared and a second two-hour session starts at 1 in the morning (Green 1998).

Bowling is making a comeback by trying to attract the next generation of bowlers. Brunswick calls it Cosmic Bowling, and AMF calls it Xtreme Bowling. Whatever the term used, the bowling industry finally realized they are not in the bowling business; they are in the entertainment business. They are competing for dollars spent on other entertainment activities such as dining out, movies, and miniature golf. Recognizing this, owners of bowling alleys are modernizing their facilities and adding attractions. Glow bowling seems to be attracting an entire new generation to the sport.

2. Bundle or unbundle current offerings to tailor them to the unique needs of different customer segments.

One characteristic of many service offerings is the ability to easily add or delete service features without dramatically changing the cost structure of the overall service. Consequently, many service features can be bundled together or unbundled to address the specific requirements of distinct customer segments. Service programs that offer "Silver, Gold, and Platinum" levels of service are examples of companies seeking to offer tailored bundles of services that appeal to different customer segments. Bundling and unbundling services can be an effective way of revitalizing more mature service offerings and increasing penetration of specific customer segments.

After seeing its membership decline to less than 40 percent of all physicians, the American Medical Association (AMA) has started to offer different levels of membership. With each increased level of membership comes additional value-added services, including journal subscriptions, discounts on financial and insurance services, educational services, and other valued offerings. The goal is to better meet the needs of distinct physician segments and, over time, increase physician membership in the AMA.

Wireless phone companies are reaching out to an underpenetrated group of security-conscious people by offering them a stripped-down wireless phone service. Although people in this segment are not currently wireless phone customers, they would consider purchasing a low-priced service contract strictly for safety reasons (e.g., the car breaks down on the highway and you need to call a repair shop, the teenager can't find his way home, etc.). For a minimal monthly fee and an exorbitant per-call charge, these customers can make emergency phone calls on their wireless telephone. The goal is to attract nonusers into the market by offering a limited service that offers an important benefit to a specific customer segment.

Extending Offerings to Increase Revenues or Maintain Price Levels

As services mature and competitive price pressures begin to erode margins, services marketers can deploy several tools for breathing life into current service offerings while maintaining existing profit margins. These tactics are primarily focused on enhancing value and differentiating services for current customers, as opposed to repositioning services to attract new customers. The six tactics available to service marketers are outlined in Figure 8.1.

Adding New Features or Applying Value-Added Technologies

Using the techniques described in Chapter 9 (Inventing New Value-Added Offerings), service marketers can uncover customers' unmet

Figure 8.1 **Approaches to Extending Current Service Offerings**

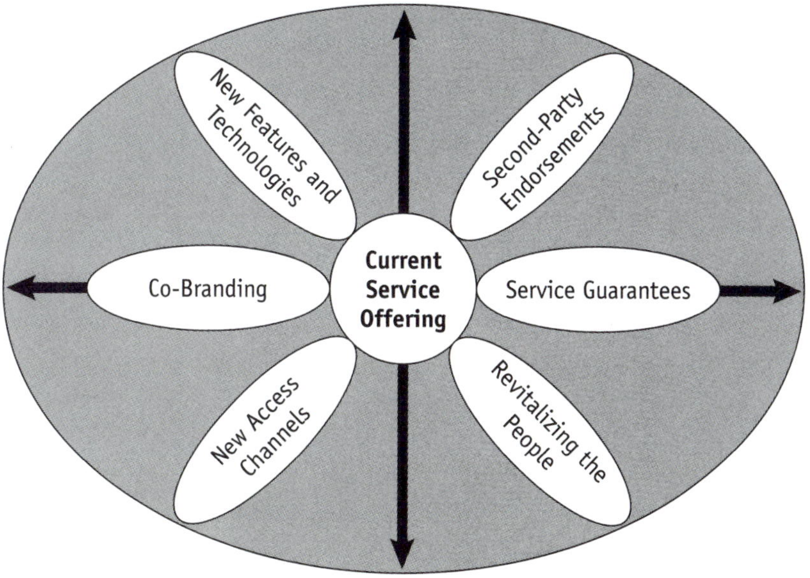

needs—desired benefits, if you will, that can be delivered by enhancing existing services. Although delivering these new benefits results in higher costs to the organization, their intention is to help a company maintain or increase prices in order to fend off margin erosion.

Marriott has become a master at enhancing their existing services. They were quick to respond to customers' needs for room add-ons such as in-room irons, coffeemakers, and phone connections for computer hookups. By being on the leading edge of enhancing their rooms and continually addressing important unmet needs of target customers, Marriott keeps its core service offering vital and differentiated.

Other service providers have found ways to apply new technologies that solve unmet customer needs and breathe life into the company's core service offering. Hertz recently launched its NeverLost system in select cities and cars. The NeverLost system uses Global Positioning System (GPS) satellite technology to help travelers find their way around unfamiliar cities. After the customer identifies their desired destination, the system determines the customer's current location and calculates the fastest or most direct route to their destination. The NeverLost system solves an important customer problem—it eliminates the need to get directions and guides customers to the appropriate route so they can reach their destination even if they take a wrong turn. This system enables Hertz to differentiate their core service offering from that of competitors and, thereby, enables Hertz to maintain higher prices and keep margins from eroding.

Co-branding with Complementary Partners

As service offerings become highly competitive and undifferentiated, one approach for breaking away from the pack is to co-brand services with complementary companies. Co-branding can provide customers with an additional reason to select one particular provider when everything else offered by competitors seems the same.

For example, Citibank and American Airlines breathed new life into the credit card business by co-branding the Citibank Aadvantage Visa card. Citibank card members earn one frequent flier mile for each dollar of purchases made using the card. In the highly competitive credit card market, Citibank has attracted customers who are more likely to remain loyal and who tend to have high monthly credit card purchases—oftentimes for business expenses. American draws their customers in further by helping them advance in frequent flier miles. Both companies benefit—and so do customers.

The Internet is creating intricate webs of co-branded offerings. DigitalWork, an Internet company focused on the business needs of small companies, has co-branded with the U.S. Chamber of Commerce, IBM, @Home, and others to help distribute its offerings. The U.S. Chamber of Commerce, IBM, and @Home bring credibility to and additional distribution muscle for DigitalWork's offerings. DigitalWork brings a suite of proven services for small businesses, objectivity as an independent provider, and a focus on delivering these e-commerce services through an on-line, Internet channel. This in turn provides goodwill and value-added offerings for @Home, IBM, and the U.S. Chamber of Commerce in the eyes of their customers.

Extending Delivery Channels

One way to differentiate current services is to provide additional methods or more convenient points of access for customers. Charles Schwab has continued to expand its delivery channels to increase customer convenience and provide the customer-preferred channels of access for different types of services. Schwab was the first broker to offer four different forms of access to their services: telephone, Internet, e-mail, and branch offices. These channel alternatives have helped Schwab remain differentiated in the highly competitive, discount brokerage services market.

New delivery channels can provide more than just enhanced benefits for current customers. New segments of customers (e.g., the technology-savvy customer who might prefer on-line access) can be attracted, and the cost to serve certain segments of customers can even be reduced (e.g., increase the amount of customer self-service in certain channels).

Revitalizing Your People

Over time, service delivery people tend to become complacent. They may fall behind in keeping their skill sets current, or fail to respond to changes in customer expectations.

Some managed-care organizations have started to send doctors to school to polish their bedside manners. As health maintenance organizations (HMOs), health plans, and provider groups vie for patients in today's competitive managed-care marketplace, some have realized they need to help doctors improve their communication skills. According to the *Wall Street Journal*, patient satisfaction surveys have uncovered widespread resentment toward doctors. In fact, studies show a poor bedside manner increases the risk of malpractice lawsuits. So doctors by the thousands are taking courses to improve their interpersonal skills and their ability to express empathy with patients and garner their trust.

Launching Service Guarantees

Service guarantees can be a powerful differentiator, because they communicate certain quality standards to customers. In the absence of other tangible cues about a company's quality of service, guarantees minimize the purchase risk and attendant uncertainty among customers. They also help a company's employees focus on a clear set of measurable standards, thereby increasing the likelihood the guarantees will be fulfilled. While it may appear service guarantees can be easily copied, in reality competitors may find them difficult to replicate if the appropriate service delivery system is not in place.

Beyond the Blockbuster Video example given at the beginning of this chapter, a variety of companies across service industries have effectively employed service guarantees. FedEx was the first to promise their packages would "absolutely, positively" get there overnight. They were the first to purchase their own fleet of planes to ensure this promise. Hampton Inn offers a 100 percent satisfaction guarantee or your money back. CarMax was the first major used-car dealer to offer a thirty-day warranty on their cars. The greater the perceived purchase risk, the more impact service guarantees are likely to have.

Securing Second-Party Endorsements

When a company's promotions get stale and repetitive, second-party endorsements from credible sources can breathe new life into a service offering by enhancing credibility. Such endorsements are particularly applicable to expertise-based services—those services that require great individual expertise in their delivery (e.g., consulting services, legal services, health care services, etc.). A well-placed article in the *Harvard Business Review*, a speech at a major industry trade show, an interview on *Nightline*, or a public-relations related mention in the *Wall Street Journal* can make a consulting firm's phones ring off the hooks! Similarly, endorsements by widely respected consumer advocate organizations such as *Consumer Reports* or J.D. Power & Associates can increase a company's credibility and trust in the eyes of customers. Second-party endorsements can renew a company's ability to maintain price levels in the face of intense competition.

Locking In Customers

When a service is new and few competitive offerings exist, customers will seek out a particular provider (assuming the new service solves an important problem and delivers value). Since customers have few (if any) choices, customer acquisition becomes the primary focus—get people to try the service. As a service offering becomes more mature and undifferentiated, investments that increase customer loyalty and retention can pay off. Research across many service industries has shown the value of retaining a customer usually far outweighs the cost of acquiring a new customer. And small increases in customer retention can result in dramatic profit increases.

Six types of investments can help create barriers to competition and make it more difficult for customers to leave (see Figure 8.2, page 132). A company must weigh the cost-benefit of each approach in order to select the one(s) most appropriate to its situation. How great is the investment? Some techniques require significant, ongoing investments in information technology. How dramatic an impact will the investment have on customer loyalty? Some techniques can offer extremely compelling benefits that make it difficult for customers to leave.

Giving Away the Tangible Service Enablers

Chapter 10 discusses service enablers in more detail. Enablers are tools, techniques, or approaches that allow a service to be performed

Figure 8.2 **Creating Competitive Barriers**

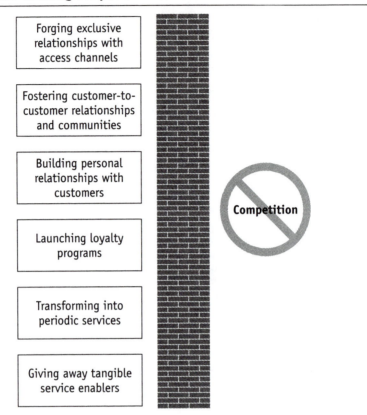

properly or that enhance the service performance. At ServiceMaster's institutional cleaning business, for example, the service enablers include special mops that increase cleaning speed and reduce strain on employees.

Giving away the tangible service enablers can enhance customer loyalty in two ways: they can make a service more convenient for the customer or create switching barriers due to retraining time and cost required to learn another company's enablers. For example, FedEx was the first overnight delivery company to give away software that made package pickup and billing more convenient. Once assimilated and in place, the software created somewhat of a switching barrier because of the training time required to learn another company's software.

Transforming One-Time Service Transactions into Periodic Services

Many services are one-time in nature. Customers purchase them, receive the service, but are left with no compelling reason to come back to the same company next time. However, some services can be transformed from a one-time event to a periodic service that creates a tie between customer and company. Start by understanding how your service fits into a longer-term series of related purchases a customer may make or activities they may undertake. Creatively explore ways you could change the terms or features of your service to provide a compelling reason to get the customer back in the future.

A few years ago, automotive repair companies began to explore a new approach to customer retention. They started by acknowledging that customers viewed their auto repair service as a one-time event—if a car needs maintenance or repair, you get it fixed and move on. However, the automotive service companies knew customers needed on-going auto repair services over the life of their vehicles. Sears was one of the first national automotive service chains to create lifetime services, such as lifetime alignments and lifetime lube-oil-filter services. These services changed the terms of the agreement from a one-time service to a periodic service that offered customers a benefit for coming back to Sears. Compared to what they would spend over the life of their car, customers get a tangible benefit. Up front, they pay a reduced, fixed amount for a guarantee of lifetime service. Sears benefits by increasing the likelihood customers will return to one of their stores. Each time the customer returns, Sears gets an opportunity to inspect the customer's car, identify additional auto repair needs, and be the one to service those needs.

Launching Loyalty Programs

Frequent-customer programs, made famous by the airline and hotel industries, have infiltrated a wide variety of service industries. Fast-food and coffee chains (e.g., Subway, Seattle's Best), grocery and drug stores (e.g., Jewel/Osco's Preferred card), credit cards (e.g., the Discover card), telephone companies, and many others have launched a variety of loyalty programs. With these programs, a customer typically builds a "credit" for each purchase. As certain levels are reached, this credit may be redeemed for discounts on future purchases, free services, or other valuable incentives.

Frequent-customer programs can require substantial investments. Information technology investments are often needed to assign individual account numbers, track customer behavior, and report account status on a regular basis. Customer service representatives are needed to handle incoming inquiries about account status. Auditing and error correction functions must be performed. The benefit of these programs is that they tend to lock customers in to a particular provider over a long period of time.

Other programs are much simpler and less expensive to administer. A customer receives a card, and each time the customer makes a purchase, the card is stamped. After the card is full, it can be redeemed for free or discounted services. While easy and inexpensive to execute, these programs typically provide only short-term incentive to purchase from a particular company.

Building Personal Relationships with Customers

Individual employees can motivate customers to return to the same provider. Over time, an employee gets to know the customer and understand the customer's individual needs. A familiar face and a predictable experience provides comfort; the customer feels more like a person than a number. In addition, employees feel more accountable and tend to deliver higher-quality service when they know the customer. Personal relationships develop that benefit both the customers and the employees.

For business-to-business services, relationship building is often built into the selling and account management process. Employees are trained in the art of relationship management, and not only are encouraged but also are measured and compensated on their effectiveness in this area. Accounting firms and consulting firms identify a partner-in-charge for major clients, responsible for deepening existing relationships and fostering new senior management relationships. Rarely, however, are individual accountants or consultants encouraged to develop relationships with their middle management counterparts in the organization. Some firms even view this activity as a detriment to their objectivity and integrity. It is these middle management relationships, however, that can provide staying power for an accounting or consulting firm. As middle managers get promoted or move on to another company, they become key decision-makers in purchasing professional services.

Some large consumer service companies are also trying to establish more personal customer-employee links. For example, some service companies are creating sophisticated customer databases that track information on individual customer purchases and needs. As a result, anyone in the company can quickly come up to speed on an individual customer. Other companies are enhancing call-routing capabilities in order to route a customer to a particular customer service representative each time the customer calls. Over time, the employee and customer build rapport and the customer's needs are better served. With both of these approaches, service companies are wise to start with their highest-volume customers first. These customers are typically most at risk, and the benefits of retaining their business can help justify the required investments.

Fostering Customer-to-Customer Relationships and Communities

A difficult but powerful technique for encouraging customer loyalty comes from fostering customer-to-customer relationships. The goal is to create an environment where customers benefit by having other customers use the same provider. As a result, customers are encouraged not only to keep coming back, but also to act as an extended sales force in referring or signing up other customers. Everyone is better off—the customers receive mutual benefits, and the provider receives more loyal customers.

MCI's Friends and Family program was a classic example of this technique. Customers received discounts if they made calls to other MCI customers designated as their friends or family members. The program encouraged customers to sign other people up with MCI so everyone could save more money. Customers were happy with the savings, and MCI had more loyal customers. Why didn't other long-distance phone companies follow suit? The general public wasn't aware of the internal information systems required to pull this off. In reality, of the major long-distance carriers, only MCI's billing system was sophisticated enough to track and bill customers in this way. Other long-distance carriers would have to make major investments to replicate MCI's capability.

Internet companies are at the cutting edge of creating virtual communities that build customer-to-customer connections and keep people coming back to the same place. Powerful connections occur when customers (members) start to contribute their own content to the site. Over time, a rich database of member content develops, and all customers are better off as they benefit from the content provided by others. Although creating customer-to-customer connections may not result in immediate revenues, these connections encourage longer-term loyalty to a site. Amazon.com encourages customers to submit book reviews that can be viewed by all members. Parentsoup.com provides forums for people to provide their parenting perspectives and to submit questions to get input from other parents. At the Motley Fool, members contribute insights about publicly traded companies. This information is particularly helpful for investors in smaller public companies, since oftentimes very little information or insights exist on the financial health of these companies.

Forging Exclusive Relationships with Access Channels

A final technique for locking in customers can be achieved by tying up access channels through exclusivity arrangements or by simply being first. Some access channels find it cost prohibitive or overly complicated to align themselves with multiple service providers. Consequently, they pick one provider, and customers are exposed only to that provider, a great advantage.

Enterprise Rent-A-Car has forged strong relationships with automotive repair companies, car dealers, and body shops. They even have their own people on-site at larger dealers and repair shops. Enterprise got there first and locked up the access channels. Customers at many auto repair shops and dealers are only presented with one option—Enterprise. Other rental car companies that want to copy Enterprise's strategy will find it difficult to muscle their way in on Enterprise's turf.

Supporting a Full-Line Offering Strategy

A fourth and final objective in revitalizing current service offerings is to support a full-line offering strategy. To the extent that the company's key point of differentiation comes from offering a full line of services, then differentiation of each individual service offering may not be possible or required. In these instances, the goal of revitalization is to enhance margins by selectively reducing investments in the individual "commodity" services. As a result, individual service offerings maintain an acceptable level of profitability, while still contributing to the full-line strategy.

For Kinko's, bulk copying services have become a commodity. Customers can choose any number of copy centers to get inexpensive copies made. Prices have fallen dramatically, and copy services are no longer major profit generators. However, copy services are still an integral part of what many people need when they go to Kinko's. Therefore, copy services remain an important part of Kinko's new strategy of being a full line office services company—as stated in their new tagline, "A New Way to Office." To improve margins on copy services, Kinko's has taken several innovative steps. First, they have worked to eliminate labor costs by making copying as self-serve as possible—customers do most of the work. Second, Kinko's investments are focused on reducing the overall life cycle costs of the equipment. They make purchases with a close eye on the long-term costs associated with toner replacement, routine maintenance, and equipment repairs. Finally, Kinko's reduced the overall space in their stores allocated to copy services. Other higher margin, value-added services get greater prominence in the store and in Kinko's customer communications. As a result of these innovations, Kinko's maximizes its investments in "required" commodity services.

Eliminating Service Offerings

Eventually, services reach a very mature phase in their life cycle and can no longer be "propped up" through revitalization efforts. They enter a virtually irreversible decline. One of the most difficult decisions a service company will ever make is killing an existing offering in the marketplace. After all, customers have bought it in the past, and some continue to buy it. "Won't we upset our customers if we stop offering this service?" "What will happen to our reputation?" "Will we ever come up with something better with which to replace it?"

At first, companies seek ways around killing a mature service. For a while, they can enhance profitability by focusing on certain customer segments, eliminating some features, cutting costs, or sometimes even charging a premium to those customers willing to pay it. However, these efforts still lead only to reduced revenues and profits over the long run. The service offering is dying a slow death.

Companies adept at following the advice offered in Chapter 9— Invent New Services—will find it easier to eliminate current offerings. The reason? They have a full pipeline of customer-desired offerings just waiting to be launched. The best way to say "No" to current service offerings is to say "Yes" to something different and even more attractive. Without anything new and better in the pipeline, companies find it difficult to kill services they have in the market. So the best approach to killing tired services is creating new, vital services in their place that solve intense customer problems. Chapter 9 offers a proven approach to addressing this challenge.

Conclusion

Services tend to be more easily duplicated than products, ultimately resulting in perceived parity in the marketplace. As customers become unable to distinguish between different offerings, price becomes a more important influence in making purchase decisions. Margins get squeezed and profits suffer.

To revitalize and keep them fresh and valued in the eyes of customers, services need a continual boost. Such revitalization efforts will extend the lives of existing services, and in turn will enable service market leaders to reap superior profits on their services for a longer period of time. Specifically, existing services can enjoy longer, more profitable lives by:
- repositioning them to expand the customer base
- extending them to improve revenues and margins from current customers by increasing the value delivered

- bolstering them to lock in customers and increase loyalty
- expanding them to provide a full line of services

Don't let services suffer an early grave. Keep them vibrant and profitable through frequent revitalization. Eventually, however, services must be totally reinvented. In the words of Kenny Rogers, "You've got to know when to hold 'em, know when to fold 'em, know when to walk away, and know when to run." We turn to this topic next.

CHAPTER 9

Invent New Services

FOR MORE THAN TWENTY-FIVE YEARS, KINKO'S has dominated the copying business. During the mid-1990s, the company made a revolutionary positioning move from being mere twenty-four-hour copying centers to being, for independent business people, "Your Branch Office." A few years later, they continued to evolve their promise to "A New Way to Office." Kinko's continuous evolution serves as a powerful testament to the strategic importance of innovation and differentiation in a changing marketplace. For Kinko's, every three to four years they need to dramatically redefine the overall benefits being delivered to customers.

Kinko's evolution started in the early 1990s, when they abandoned much of their duplication services centered around colleges and universities, specifically the "Courseworks" packets. This market had become a commodity. Kinko's shifted away from being a twenty-four-hour photocopying business. They focused on delivering a new service experience—a business person's branch office. Management believed it could lead and expand the industry by delivering, on a national basis, high-quality, one-stop business support services. Kinko's decided to target small office and home office professionals and provide a full array of basic business support services under one roof, conveniently located, competitively priced, and typically open twenty-four hours a day. They wanted small business customers to experience a full range of services designed specifically for them—services that reduced customers' overhead expenses and gave them access to the advantages typically enjoyed only by large companies.

In order for their new strategy to succeed, senior management committed to constantly listening to customers and then successfully creating and launching new services. They built new Kinko's locations with more square footage than in prior years to create true business centers. They introduced a full range of services, dramatically expanded the number of locations, and solidified service quality across offices. They introduced services such as faxing, computer-time rentals, mailboxes, overnight mail services, desktop publishing, work areas, and printing.

The work of innovation, however, is never done. Kinko's one-stop services once again became standard offerings in a rapidly maturing market. By the late 1990s, these services became expected by customers as new competitors such as Mail Boxes, Etc. and Office Depot realized that they could expand their businesses by offering services to small office and home office professionals. As competition followed, Kinko's had to push the branch office concept even further by introducing new value-adding services. These have included:

- entering into alliances such as a videoconferencing arrangement with Sprint
- creating specific services for niche market segments such as hotel business centers in selected locations
- increasing convenience for customers by adding FedEx, Airborne Express, and UPS drop-off boxes inside their stores, with the latest possible pickup times in their area
- introducing new technology-based services such as the "KinkoNet" electronic networking service that allows users to hook up with a Kinko's location, download their document, and choose a service

These innovations have helped Kinko's extend the branch office concept they created and launched years earlier.

The Kinko's process is a "grass-roots" approach that takes ideas directly from the customers. At headquarters in California, an operations and product development committee is responsible for developing new services and researching new equipment. On a national level, approximately 400 partners and owners gather every year for brainstorming meetings. Each partner usually brings one or two ideas that have resulted from direct contact with and formal feedback from local customers. While new services get launched on a national scale, each individual Kinko's location must prioritize and assess its capabilities to deliver new services. For example, not all locations provide specialty services such as videoconferencing.

But now for the tough question: How far can Kinko's extend its concept of "A New Way to Office"? There comes a time when the overall service experience created for customers does not produce enough differentiation and value-added benefits for customers to distinguish it from the competition. And, when this happens, the company does not grow and produce satisfactory profits. That time has come for Kinko's. The future for Kinko's is to become unbounded by physical stores; to stop being a retailer where customers must go to them. They need a new philosophy that says, "We go to our customers." This will transform them into more of a business services provider. The retail stores may become more like regional operations centers as salespeople, on-line computer services, pickup and delivery services, and on-customer-site presence will become the point of interface with customers. Customers will rely on Kinko's for ideas and comprehensive solutions for their needs, enabling them to be more effective and efficient business professionals. This is an exciting future for small businesses and for Kinko's. The first part of this future was unfolded with the launch of "Digital Printing" and a whole campaign encouraging Kinko's customers to "Go Digital." Now it will require a significant number of new service innovations over the coming years in order to bring tangible value to customers with this new approach.

At the foundation of Kinko's strategic innovation success is a deeply felt belief by managers that "Our customers are the most creative and intelligent people. They drive what we do." Kinko's managers truly "walk the talk" of a customer-driven philosophy. This philosophy drives truly great innovative organizations to develop value-adding new service concepts—over and over again. Listening to customers is the spark to everything Kinko's does to continue its market leadership. Listening enables them to innovate ahead of competitors and continue to lead the industry. The challenge felt most deeply by those in the marketing department is to address their customers' problems and needs with unique benefits that are delivered through current and new services.

The strategy of innovating new services is a fundamental one for service market leaders. This chapter provides an approach for developing a continuous stream of new services.

New Service Innovations

If service companies stop with their oppositioning strategy and do not develop new services, they find themselves reliving the old Wendy's commercial with customers asking "Where's the Beef?" Simply put, the beef is what customers will get. It is the specific benefit they will get as part of a unique experience they will have with the company. "The beef" is the service concept that needs to be invented, reinvented, evolved, or bolstered—depending on the changed needs of customers and the competitive environment.

But what do service innovations look like? Below are some new services that have had significant impacts in their markets:

Discount brokerage	Branded maid service
Televised home shopping	Eyeglasses in one hour
All-sports TV channel	1-900 phone entertainment
Overnight mail delivery	On-line PC home services
ATM banking	24-hour home security
Frequent flyer award miles	Pager service
Pizza delivered to home	Data center outsourcing
All-suite hotels	Consumer auto leases
Children's day-care centers	Warehouse clubs
Wireless phone service	

This list represents the final results of what service companies hope to achieve with their new service innovation efforts. We can all recognize new concepts after they have been widely accepted. The common phrase that most customers use when they discover one is "Now that is a good idea!" Similarly, all organizations have the desire to create new benefits for their customers. But while the desire is there, the inventing process is often a combination of raw-idea overload and process idleness. Service organizations need to learn how to bridge the gap from wishful intent to intentional invention.

New service innovations should focus on the benefits customers will derive from the service experience. And there are different service experiences for different customers. A distinction should also be made between the experience itself and the service "platform" that enables the experience to occur. For example, Marriott Hotels provides a variety of experiences for different customers that go beyond room rentals. Marriott leverages different platforms. These may include dining on the road (for business travelers, with the hotel restaurant as the platform), business meetings (for business groups, with convention rooms as the platform), marriage celebrations (for newlyweds, with the ballroom as the platform), and husband-and-wife retreats (for married couples, with weekend packages as the platform). These are different experiences desired by different customers. So a key aspect of new service innovation is defining the desired experience and resulting benefits for targeted groups of customers.

There are many reasons why service organizations, in particular, seem to do a poor job of creating new service innovations:

- Development teams lack the knowledge required to translate directional growth strategies into definitions of specific future benefits.
- Management wrongfully thinks that innovations only come in one size—usually either one-offs designed for only one customer, or patentable breakthroughs. Either case sets up the wrong mind-set.
- There is an underlying belief that innovation should happen in a research group somewhere and that it only occurs once in a while.
- The organization lacks a formal development process and wrongfully starts the process with brainstorming a lot of ideas that have no connection to customer needs.

To overcome these shortcomings, five principles should be applied for successfully creating new service innovations.

1. Link new service concepts to the innovation strategy.
2. Pursue a portfolio of new service types.

3. Solve well-defined customer problems.
4. Follow a customer-inspired and customized development process.
5. Pursue new service concepts continuously.

Link New Service Concepts to the Innovation Strategy

Service companies should pursue new services that are strategically linked to the company's directional growth strategies and are consistent with the needs of targeted market segments. They do this by ensuring all new services link to the innovation strategy (from Chapter 7). At a strategic level, companies should identify desired service offerings (or at least a conceptual description of the future offerings) that will satisfy new service strategic roles and fit the new service vision. Specifically, new services must align with the company's growth and differentiation strategies and must satisfy core business objectives such as addressing future customer needs, responding to industry evolution, responding to competitor advances, and taking advantage of new technologies.

Let's turn to an example. Kinder-Care offers high-quality, reputable day care for young children in a familiar and safe environment. Kinder-Care is to day-care centers what Blockbuster Video was to the video rental market: the first national player in a fragmented, largely mom-and-pop industry. The difference is that while Blockbuster distributes a very specific product, Kinder-Care positions itself as a trusted, regulated provider of child-care services—one with many advantages over the average day-care center. This focus and the overall increased demand for child-care services helped Kinder-Care to experience tremendous initial growth.

However, in the late 1980s, instead of strategically innovating its maturing core business, management turned to acquisitions and diversification as the means for growth. Concurrently, competition from other national chains, such as Le Petite Academy and from stronger local centers increased dramatically. These two factors contributed to Kinder-Care's near miss with bankruptcy in 1993.

This "wake-up call" served to rally the ingenuity and inventiveness of Kinder-Care employees to create new service concepts. They started by refocusing on Kinder-Care's core service benefit of offering education and day care for young children. They then applied their op-positioning strategy of being "a trusted provider of whole-child development in the absence of parents." Kinder-Care's recent communications emphasize the personal relationships and demonstrate the array of professionally supervised and enriching activities that children pursue during their stay. Finally, service concepts now include new, larger centers in metropolitan areas (called "community centers"), on-site child-care services for corporations (called "Kinder-Care at Work"), and new before- and after-school service options for six- to twelve-year-olds (called "Kid's Choice"), featuring a unique environment for kids of that age.

Management's new focus has created a tight linkage between the overall business strategy and the specific new service offerings that produce benefits for customers. In addition, this onslaught of internally generated, strategically aligned innovations enabled Kinder-Care to experience several years of rising profits.

Suppose you are the president of one of the country's largest chains of movie theaters. Because of the dramatic growth of home videos and the lack of innovation within the movie theater industry, the number of people going to movies has been on the decline. Considering the glut of movie theaters, significant price competition, and disloyal movie patrons, earning a profit has become considerably more difficult. This competitive environment has caused you to be more open to new service innovations.

After reading Chapter 6 of this book, you acknowledge that competing on the movie titles and pricing specials merely keeps you in a product business and not appropriately oppositioned to your nearby competitor. Therefore, you set a course to transition your business to become a provider of service experiences to patrons under the unique banner "enhanced environments for watching movies." To deliver on this promise, new service concepts must be developed. You decide to plot a strategic view of the new service concepts from two perspectives. First, you look at the degree customers value particular benefits. These benefits can be grouped into either "expected supplementary services" or "differentiating value-adding services." Second, examine the role each new service concept fulfills by deciding whether it satisfies a requisite (more defensive) or expansive (more offensive) role.

Figure 9.1 **Movie Theatre Strategic Innovation Chart**

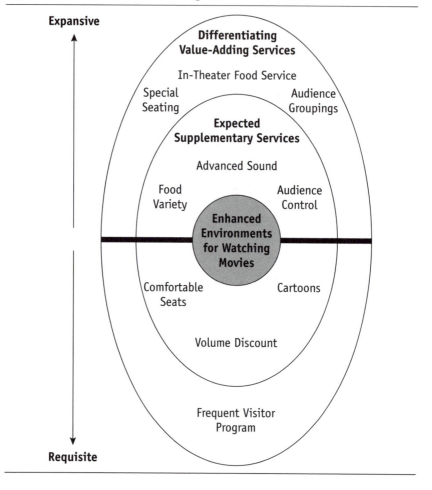

Figure 9.1 is an example of a strategic chart you might construct for a typical ten-screen movie theater location.

Pursue a Portfolio of New Service Types

As highlighted in Chapter 7, creating service innovations means creating *failures*. Therefore, it is essential to pursue a portfolio of new service projects. The types of projects in a portfolio should be multi-

Figure 9.2 **Movie Theater New Service Portfolio**

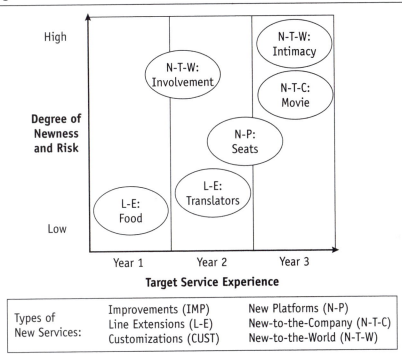

Types of New Services:

	Improvements (IMP)	New Platforms (N-P)
	Line Extensions (L-E)	New-to-the-Company (N-T-C)
	Customizations (CUST)	New-to-the-World (N-T-W)

dimensional along the following lines: First, the portfolio composition should be influenced by considerations for both expansive and requisite strategic roles, as well as differentiating and expected services. Second, portfolios should have a range of types of new services—including improvements, line extensions, customizations, platform enablers, new-to-the-company and new-to-the-world services. Defining services in this way helps classify their degree of newness and the degree of risk inherent in the new concept. As a rule of thumb, consider establishing three-year goals of allocating 20 percent of resources to the new-to-the-world and new-to-the-company categories, 40 percent of resources to the line-extension and new platform categories, and 40 percent of resources to the improvement and cost-reduction categories.

The project portfolio (see Figure 9.2) for the hypothetical movie theater example focuses on the desired expansive roles and benefits that are from the differentiating value-adding services dimension.

Figure 9.3 Movie Theater Project Plans

Type:	Line extension
Idea:	Fast-food meals that can be eaten in the theater during the movie.
Investment:	$100 K
Market Launch:	Year 1
Type:	New-to-the-world
Idea:	Increased involvement by patrons with movie through sight and sound enhancements and stage actors.
Investment:	$3 million
Market Launch:	Year 2
Type:	New platform
Idea:	Tiered seating and prices and improved side seating.
Investment:	$2 million
Market Launch:	Year 2
Type:	Line extension
Idea:	Headsets for translations into Spanish, French, English, etc.
Investment:	$500 K
Market Launch:	Year 2
Type:	New-to-the-world
Idea:	Environment of high intimacy between patrons for romantic and drama movies.
Investment:	$5 million
Market Launch:	Year 3
Type:	New-to-the-company (with MGM)
Idea:	New sound and special effects designed into movie film that is unleashed by special technology in theater.
Investment:	$5 million
Market Launch:	Year 3

Once a directional project portfolio has been developed, it is important to develop further descriptions and plans for each project. Figure 9.3 shows the project plans for the movie theater portfolio.

Solve Well-Defined Customer Problems

In order to create breakthrough service experiences, there must be a unique, specific benefit that customers want. But how do service companies determine what customers want? And how do companies lead customers to discover what they really want? Most people didn't really know they wanted overnight mail delivery, frequent flyer miles, wireless phones, or lawn care services until these services were introduced to them. The one absolute essential is to engage in a creation process that begins and ends by solving a well-defined problem of a target group of customers. It is that simple. Southwest Airlines began by solving the problem of getting people to other Texas cities faster than by car and doing it cost-effectively. Unfortunately, most service organizations get bogged down with too many internally generated and breakthrough-sounding ideas that have no basis in marketplace reality.

An example is the credit card industry. Try to think of all the credit card innovations produced in the last ten years. These include different levels of cards (Gold, Platinum), partnerships with airlines on frequent flyer miles, travel insurance, prewritten paper checks sent to customers, affinity cards for specialty groups, and cash back on purchases. Looking at this list, one would conclude that these "innovations" have really been marketing promotions or feature enhancements. Such enhancements can revitalize and breathe life into an existing service (as discussed in Chapter 8). However, none are truly new, market-driven service innovations.

What is missing? The innovations that uniquely address the customers' new financial needs. Most Americans have credit cards as (a) an alternative form of payment, (b) a source of funds in an emergency, (c) a way to buy things on credit, and (d) a convenient way to buy larger items. Let's focus on innovating (c), the overall service experience or benefit of "buying things on credit."

If the central benefit that credit card issuers provide is a revolving, unsecured, limited line of credit, then new service innovation would not be complete unless a new solution relative to this benefit is being created. New solutions are derived from five generic problem categories that can apply to most all service situations. These are solutions that:

1. Prevent the problem
2. Solve part of the problem
3. Solve the problem differently
4. Solve a related problem
5. Solve a broader problem

Figure 9.4 **Five Problem Categories for New Service Innovation—Credit Card Example**

Problem Categories	Concept Innovations
Prevents the Problem "I have a problem with carrying and losing the card."	*Objective:* eliminate the physical card *Solution:* no more card verification, just voice and fingerprint recognition activated with new devices *New Benefit:* **higher security**
Solves Part of the Problem "My card is not accepted at some of the stores I want to shop at."	*Objective:* offer nonparticipating merchants an incentive *Solution:* bank issued and guaranteed "bank bucks" that the customer can give to a merchant as compensation for taking the risk of credit card acceptance *New Benefit:* **increased card acceptance by stores**
Solves the Problem Differently "I want to carry a balance from month to month but at a lower interest rate."	*Objective:* replace the unsecured line of credit *Solution:* a secured line of credit based on their home—a home equity credit card *New Benefit:* **lower interest rates**
Solves a Related Problem "To better manage our budget, I would like a way to change the spending limit monthly."	*Objective:* offer changeable credit limits *Solution:* an internet accessed or 1-800 number program in which the credit limit can be increased or decreased up to twelve times per year *New Benefit:* **personal control over credit limits**
Solves a Broader Problem "I hate having so many different types of short-term debt or loans with the bank."	*Objective:* tie revolving debt, auto loans, and personal loans together *Solution:* a preapproved personal line of credit, accessed through credit card and checks, that automatically converts to three-year payback schedule with lower interest rates on purchases over $5,000 *New Benefit:* **total borrowing experience easier**

Within each of these problem categories, many different needs of target customer segments can be identified. Needs themselves come in three varieties:

a. Unsatisfied needs: customers are not able to get the "right" solution to their problem. This situation typically occurs when current providers offer relatively low-quality service or because an identified customer need has shifted from one year to the next ahead of providers' ability or willingness to respond. Solving these needs tends to generate expected, supplementary new services.

b. Unmet needs: customers have an identified need but find no provider available to fulfill it. This situation typically occurs because customers have been performing the activity themselves in-house or because new environmental conditions have recently created the need.

c. Unknown needs: customers cannot easily articulate solutions to their problems that might come from some outside source. Solving these needs tends to generate differentiating, value-adding new services.

For the hypothetical credit card example in Figure 9.4 (page 152), one need for each problem category is shown in the form of a customer quote. The right-hand column then shows what new and innovative concepts could be created to solve the particular problem. This is inventing at its best.

Inventing new concepts or experiences that bring new benefits to customers need not be thought of as some mystical process for only "creative" people. In reality, it is a very analytical, problem-solving endeavor. The essential ingredient is to begin the process by determining the customer problem that must be solved and determining the range of alternative solutions desired. Since Charles Schwab invented the concept of discount brokerage, his organization has worked tirelessly over the years to uncover and understand the financial and investment problems faced by target customers. Today, Schwab has successfully followed up with many new services and product solutions that customers enthusiastically embrace.

Follow a Customer-Inspired and Customizable Development Process

Successful service development requires a process that contains three elements:

1. Fully understand and define a solvable customer problem through large doses of targeted research. Customer research will also help

determine alternative solutions to the problem, develop specific aspects of the chosen solution, and design the best way to market and sell the new concept when it's ready to be released into the marketplace.

2. Acknowledge that new service development requires bringing a set of customers into the development process. Customer input provides direct feedback and access to a real-life laboratory for creating the new service concept and experience.

3. Follow a disciplined process that is appropriate for the customer environment and then customize the process to support the specific objective of the new concept being created. Chapter 12 will provide additional detail on the new service development process.

The Role of Market Research

Market research and new service development often operate like oil and vinegar. When properly integrated, they produce an experience to savor. But more often than not, they repel one another with market research being severely curtailed. A lack of adequate market research during development usually can be attributed to two things: concerns over the benefits of doing market research in the first place and inappropriate new service development research methodology.

As it relates to the first concern, justifying the benefits of doing market research in the first place, new service developers must overcome three problems:

1. Outdated, inaccurate market research at the time a new service is launched, caused by research that is conducted too far in advance of a new service introduction. Services tend to have short life cycles, which means that at the time of introduction, the market's requirements may have already evolved into a new phase.

2. Market requirements that are too broad and developed for a mass market. Rather, new services should be developed for an environment where they can be tailored at the point of delivery to create individualized experiences.

3. Fear of having the new service concept stolen by a competitor during development. This arises because services generally have low barriers to duplication or, often, short but profitable life spans.

Market research methodologies for new *product* development tend not to address these three problems. New product development processes traditionally receive input from the market at two entry points in the development process. First, after the idea-brainstorming step, the process is used for refining and validating the customer requirements of the concepts. The second point of input occurs when a complete business plan is developed and research is used for estimating market size, competitive share, ballpark pricing parameters, and the like. This traditional methodology is like a funnel that seeks broad market inputs during the early steps in development and then seeks more specific feedback later in the process—but only on "product marketing" issues.

Market research for new *service* development, however, needs input from customers throughout the creation process and a research methodology that takes into account the experiential and customer-intimate nature of services. To address these concerns and shortcomings, new service developers should consider implementing a "reverse customer research" approach. This approach is opposite to the traditional product development approach in that it generally starts with narrower market research up front from a select group of customers and experts, and then moves to more broad-based customer feedback as the new concept is being finalized. It also allows for more customer research intimacy, an essential element when creating intangible services.

The proposed reverse customer research methodology for service development can be applied in four phases—relatively simply.

- Phase 1: Conduct exploratory research with targeted customers who are considered to be experts or leading-edge thinkers. Learnings and discoveries regarding customer problems to be solved should be carried from one interview to the next.
- Phase 2: Conduct highly focused, in-depth research with a selected group of customers. It could also include core customers established as development partners.
- Phase 3: Build the mandatory business case by taking inputs from the selected group of customers and extrapolating to estimate the broader market characteristics.
- Phase 4: Conduct broad-based research to determine the total market's likelihood of purchase. This research should be conducted within three months prior to introduction and include

testing the service delivery experience, as well as its functionality, with all the targeted market segments.

Customer Participation During Development

Bringing customer opinion into the process is particularly constructive for new service developers, who must themselves become disciples of the market and zealots in solving customer problems. A customer-driven new service development process is one that allows for significant and specific customer involvement. Pursuit of a customer-involved process enables developers of new services to be close to the market and to customer requirements.

A customer-involved development process is one that establishes customers as integrated partners during all steps—from problem identification to post-launch. The first step in implementing this approach is to determine what customer-involved insights and feedback carry most impact. The following seven categories of customer feedback are most appropriate:

1. Confirm service offering requirements.
2. Assess points-of-value.
3. Test delivery experience.
4. Provide rapid learning on concept iterations.
5. Identify points-of-quality variability.
6. Analyze impact to customers' processes.
7. Develop alternative customization approaches.

In addition to determining areas that are most appropriate for in-depth customer insights and feedback, developers should clarify:

- How are customers to be involved? The approaches could range from arm's-length "we're helping each other out" arrangements to contractually bound "there is something tangible in this for both of us" agreements.
- What is the total number of customers involved? This can range from a few to hundreds.
- How extensively are customers involved? This level of involvement could range from simple responses to survey questions to regular face-to-face meetings with the new service development team.

There is no simple algorithm for combining these variables. It always depends on the specific situation. The purpose for involvement and the way customers are integrated into the development process are, however, most often driven by the following factors:

- the kind of service customer—i.e., consumer or business—and the level of their involvement in the service experience
- the degree of newness of the new service
- the market dynamics of category size, window of opportunity, competitive uniqueness, and potential impact on customer value
- the degree of intangibility and "protectability" of the new service

A development rule of thumb is that a service company should configure their customer involvement so that the company obtains a sufficient depth of insight to ensure a "proof of the service concept's value" for each individual customer. Also, a service company should ensure that they attain enough breadth of coverage to provide for "proof of the service concept" for the broader target customer segments.

Customizing the Development Process

In Chapter 12, a step-by-step process is introduced that can function as a starting point for most organizations. The point here is not to debate what are the right steps in the process, but simply to emphasize the need for having a development process. It can, of course, be customized. And what are the benefits of customizing the process? More-rapid development times, greater protection of new services, leverageable customer references at introduction, and faster experiential learning for quick enhancements and future adaptations.

Customizing the process means adjusting the type and degree of rigor based on the situation. However, it *never* means skipping steps in the process. The following two primary factors determine when to customize the new service development process:

1. the degree of "newness" of the new service, i.e., the type of new service
2. the level of investment, which indicates the degree of risk and strategic expectations of the new service under development

Figure 9.5 Customizing the New Service Development Process

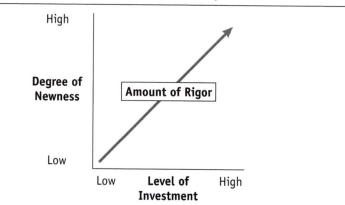

After determining when customization should occur, seven essential *how* elements, which need to be reviewed for possible modification of the rigor, apply to the service development process. These are:

1. amount of detailed documentation
2. complexity of decision-making process
3. depth of analysis
4. definition of what is to be launched
5. amount of operational, delivery, and customer testing
6. breadth and pervasiveness of research
7. amount of time needed for each step

The chart in Figure 9.5 shows the relationship between the customizing factors and elements. In general, when a truly new service is being developed (with significant investments in infrastructure and delivery), the development team's mission should be to "go slower and get it right." If the opposite is true, then "go faster and get it out" should guide the process.

Pursue New Service Concepts Continuously

New service development must be ongoing because of changing customer needs, not to mention the constant encroachment of competitors. Also, new service development must go beyond mere incremental innovations. Developers of new concepts also must recognize and plan for the certainty of failures. Risks are being taken, so failures will and need to occur.

Service commodification happens all too quickly. Customers get used to a service's unique benefit and come to expect it—for increasingly lower prices. As the degree of commodification becomes more severe, customers begin to act as though they expect the benefits to be free. (Remember the days when customers had to pay for advice from a stockbroker?)

While it may seem obvious to continually innovate when the service industry or company is maturing, the true leaders are doing this during growth cycles as well. Consider the following example. During the 1980s, gas stations that also offered limited food items gained in popularity. SuperAmerica, a subsidiary of Ashland Oil, seized upon this trend and has been continually innovating this "gas and snacks" concept ever since—so much so that both gas stations and convenience stores feel threatened.

SuperAmerica was the first convenience store to introduce a bakery (called SuperMom's), a deli, and ATMs into its stores. These have now become standards at 7-Eleven and other rival chains. SuperAmerica continually pursues concept innovations such as:

- adding more food, more variety, and more services
- evolving its service identity from gas and snacks to today's new gas station category of a hybrid convenience-store and supermarket concept
- offering fast-food brand names in its stores
- integrating Rally's fast-food restaurants into some single Super-America buildings, thus combining gasoline refueling with a drive-through restaurant
- participating as a full franchiser of some stores, like Subway, which provides for total control over the integration of the two offerings
- developing their own series of private label products

To further create this new category of "gas and food, one-stop convenience," SuperAmerica has added auto supplies, health products, and pet food to their merchandise lines. Some stores have also ventured into video rentals, compact disc sales, and pharmaceuticals, based on the specific demographics of customers being served.

It is unclear how far this trend of conglomerating "fast any-thing"—be it gas, burgers, or household staples—will go. But in the fast lane of competitive service businesses, SuperAmerica's success formula of continually innovating the definition of the new category, as well as the tangible benefits sold to customers, is a model to follow.

Conclusion

Inventing new services must become the lifeblood of every service organization that wants to grow profitably. For a daring few, it is their mantra and drive for dominating their market niche. As is discussed and illustrated in this chapter, continuously creating new service innovations can, indeed, become a process that is part and parcel of the fabric of an organization. But beyond being just a process, it must be a mind-set and a goal that people at all levels of the company understand and embrace.

CHAPTER 10

Innovate the Service Process

WHY DID BUSINESS TRAVELERS JUMP UP AND down when Marriott invented a rapid checkout service? The service saved customers time by avoiding long checkout lines in the morning. Instead, customers' bills were waiting under the door in the morning. Customers could check out by calling the front desk or pressing a sequence of buttons with the TV remote control. Or how about when Hertz invented rapid check-in with their Hertz Gold service? Now customers could save time by skipping long check-in lines and proceeding directly to their rental car. Marriott and Hertz innovated the *process* of how customers receive their service.

For service organizations, a unique, valued service concept is not enough to lock in customers over the long run. As stated before, many service concepts can be quickly replicated by competitors, resulting in spiraling prices and erosion of profit margins. One critical element in differentiating services and locking in customers for the long run is found in the *process* of delivering the service experience to customers. Market-leading service organizations use the service process as a primary source for giving customers an experience that will keep them coming back time and time again.

In product companies, innovating how the product is produced is important for cost reasons and can, in fact, lead to competitive advantage in the product itself. In general, however, and excluding environmental practices and food products, customers could care less how a product is produced as long as it delivers superior or unique benefits. Thus, differentiation for products must happen in their features, positioning, branding, new product development, distribution and customer integration. For customers, the production process is meaningless.

By contrast, services are experiences or performances waiting to happen. People, computers, facilities, equipment, scripts, and methodologies are the interconnected components of a service that stands idle until the signal is given for the performance to occur. The way in which all these components come together to form the customer's experience is called the service process. The service process is the sequence of steps before, during, and after the customer receives the service and all of the interactions that occur during each step. These steps may be almost identical for each customer (as in an automatic car wash) or quite varied and tailored to each customer (as in many consulting services). As the process unfolds, customers see some of the components, while other components do their part behind the scenes.

Consider a Broadway musical. To have the performance be a rewarding experience for the audience, each actor, singer, musician, prop, light, stagehand, speaker, microphone, etc., must work in harmony with one another—at the right time and in the right way. "At the right time" refers to the order of steps in the process. "In the right way" refers to the actual performance of each contributor. For example, did the lead singer start her solo at the right time? Did the main spotlight for the lead singer turn on immediately upon the beginning of her solo? Did the spotlight operator accurately blend the red, blue, and yellow filters into a spectacular color display during her last note? Did she excite the crowd by holding her last note for a full minute as she had talked about during rehearsal? Of course, the audience is hoping for such an exhibition. But for the producer of the show, too much creative latitude (and with it the increased chance of error) is often the biggest cause of ulcers.

All Broadway musicals attempt to create a unique, valued experience for the audience through excellence in the service process. The director orchestrates this process by carefully selecting each component, allowing for appropriate creative latitude with performers, and sequencing all of the individual performances. For this service offering, the process of the musical is arguably more important to success than the topic (i.e., the concept) of the musical.

Innovating the service process offers incredible potential for making the service experience more unique and valued by target customers.

Innovating the Service Process

Let's look at LensCrafters as an example of innovating the service process. In the late 1970s, LensCrafters' founders took advantage of deregulation in the optometry profession and changing demands for eyewear to create a truly unique and original concept. Every LensCrafters store, most of which are located in shopping malls, offers customized eyeglasses delivered in one hour. The benefit of being able to get proper fitting eyeglasses in hours (versus days) was certainly new and appealing to customers. LensCrafters' sustaining innovation occurred in the design of its service process, which was established to deliver the important benefit of speed. Customers are taken through a process that, under one roof, combines all the functions necessary to create a pair of glasses. The process emphasizes service over the tangible product of glasses. Customers experience:

- the expertise of licensed optometrists during their eye exam
- the advanced lab technology as they meet with lab technicians
- the ego fulfillment that their new glasses look great, as they interact with friendly retail employees who assist in selecting the right frame

The fact that LensCrafters has a large inventory of quality frames at reasonable prices (the frames are their products and major source of revenue) is kept in the proper perspective as a secondary benefit of the service concept and process. This is evident in LensCrafters' recent communications strategy, which shifts from stressing the convenience of the service to focusing on the people who deliver high-quality medical services. Through the years, management's commitment to innovating and delivering a high-quality service process has resulted in explosive growth and strong profit margins.

Let's look at an example of an effective service process in the medical services field. In Toronto, Canada, there is a highly innovative and successful hospital that exclusively performs hernia operations. Shortly after World War II, Dr. Earle Shouldice established Shouldice Hospital, which features the Shouldice method for hernia repair. This method is grounded in the benefit of helping patients (mostly men) recover more rapidly from surgery—patients recover in days at Shouldice versus weeks at other hospitals. Using the Shouldice method, patients literally walk away from the operating table. The slow walk of Shouldice patients is affectionately referred to as "the Shouldice Shuffle." With hernia operations at most hospitals, patients are wheeled away en route to days of recovery confined to a bed.

But Dr. Shouldice didn't stop with just the operating method. To fully solidify this service business' success, he innovated other aspects of the service process. He determined that rapid recovery occurs when both physiological and psychological elements are treated. Thus, much of the process focuses on the mental well-being of patients. It includes rapid check-in and exams; presurgery interactions with happy, recovering patients; local anesthetized surgery; recovery exercises led by encouraging nurses; and, finally, planned bonding time with fellow recovering "classmates." The innovativeness of this service process has produced much fame and good fortune for the hospital. Many of their patients rank the whole service experience as one of their most memorable. A legion of male post-hernia zealots gather every year in New York, ostensibly for a checkup but also to rebond with fellow classmates by swapping their Shouldice Shuffle stories.

In order to create service experiences that deliver value and lock in customers, companies must carefully consider two elements of the service process:

1. the design of the actual service process itself, including the steps, sequence, timing, and interactions

2. the design of the service enablers, or tools, techniques, and approaches that enable execution to happen

Designing a Service Process

Take out a blank piece of paper. On it, identify the steps of a particular service process. In doing so, you are creating a service process map. This is a powerful, strategic, simple method for determining how to deliver more unique value to customers.

A service process map graphically demonstrates the sequential flow of activities and interactions between the customer, frontline employees, support employees, and company assets. The primary goals of service process maps are to:

- demonstrate the service delivery process from the customer's point of view, and define the customer's involvement
- define all the components and interactions involved in service delivery to ensure that each adds value
- identify critical areas where service delivery may break down, so contingency and recovery plans can be developed

Figure 10.1 on page 166 illustrates the key components of a service process map.

Start by identifying and sequencing all interactions between the customer and frontline company employees. These interactions may be in-person or by phone and involve direct contact between the customer and company. Next, map the physical operations of the service that are invisible to customers—the interactions between frontline company employees and support employees. Finally, indicate employee interactions with company assets required to support the process such as important equipment, vehicles, and information databases.

For a new service, a high-level map should be created that conveys a simple understanding of the entire service delivery system. Several alternative maps may be appropriate to describe different ways the service might be delivered. The customer interface portion of each alternative can then be tested with customers to determine the optimal

Figure 10.1 Service Process Map Components*

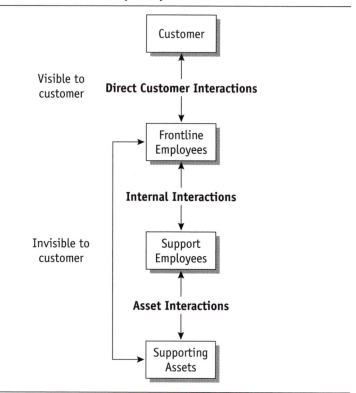

*Concepts are adapted from G. Lynn Shostack, "Service Positioning Through Structural Change," *Journal of Marketing,* January 1987.

service definition and delivery approach. Finally, subsequent maps may be developed to demonstrate this in greater detail by outlining specific activities for critical areas of the process—such as handoffs and points of customer interaction. Figure 10.2 illustrates a sample service process map for a typical restaurant experience.

In order to create something new and different, three service process design factors must be balanced. These factors are similar to the three picture-control knobs on the old television set. Each of the controls has a range of settings that adjusts either the contrast, brightness, or vertical view of the picture. Although independent of each other, they are interrelated technologies; so the three controls must be concurrently adjusted to get the picture you want.

Figure 10.2 **Service Process Map—Restaurant Experience**

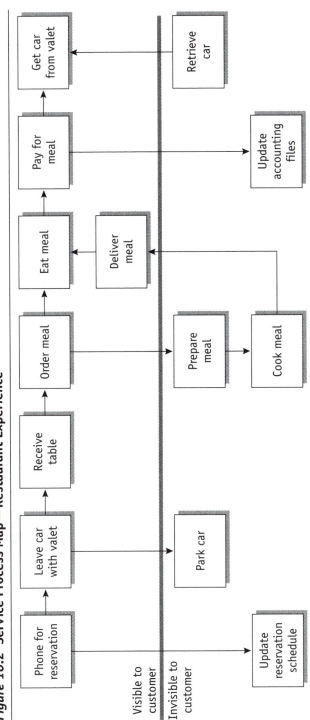

The three innovation variables in the design of service processes are:

1. the number and sequence of steps in the process
2. the points of discretion in the process where an *employee* should apply judgment or discretion (which means the outcome of that action is less controllable)
3. the predefined range of discretion within which employees are allowed to operate during the process

Innovating the Number of Steps or Sequence of Steps

The steps in a service process can be increased, decreased, or reordered to create a unique, valued service experience. For example, at Shouldice Hospital, while the steps in the process immediately before and after the actual surgery have been shortened, the number of steps in the process during recovery have been increased. The net effect makes the whole service experience feel different and better to patients. Similarly, many fast-food restaurants reduced the number of steps in the process by adding drive-through lanes. Customers "on the go" view these changes as innovative and valuable. Both increasing and decreasing the steps are sources for innovation and advantage.

And don't always assume that reducing the number of steps increases the speed of the process. If customers want speed, consider increasing the amount of self-service (e.g., pay-at-the-pump gas stations), performing steps in advance of the customer's visit (e.g., pre-chopped vegetables at Taco Bell), collecting and using information on individual customer preferences (e.g., travel profiles stored for frequent fliers), or combining steps under one roof (e.g., LensCrafters' approach).

Innovating the Points of Discretion

Acknowledging and identifying points in the service process where individual employee discretion can be applied is often a major step toward bringing service organizations back into the *service* business. Companies that have taken their quality initiatives too far usually have removed almost all discretion in the service process, under the false notion that standardization leads to profitability. This may be true in the short run, but it systematically and institutionally extracts the opportunities for innovation and neutralizes the employees' skills and experience in creative satisfaction of customers' needs.

Similar to altering the number of steps in the process, strategically innovating the points of discretion means either increasing or decreasing the number of places where discretion is desired. When this type of change creates a noticeable difference relative to competitors, it can register as a point of difference for customers.

For example, at Shouldice Hospital discretion is given to the doctors and nurses regarding their encouragement to patients to get off the operating table and walk back to their rooms. At the same time, discretion is taken away from the doctors regarding the actual procedure of the operation. At Southwest Airlines, discretion is given to customers regarding what seat they select as they board the airplane as well as to flight attendants regarding the amount of humor they use during their announcements and safety instructions. At Walt Disney Theme Parks, the employees are called actors because whether they are serving food or cleaning the grounds, they are expected to use their judgment and personality when interacting with customers. Disney employees are encouraged to make sure customers have a positive, memorable experience. If there are no points of discretion within a service process, then the service experience would be completely standardized.

Some industries are being forced to add discretion to their service process in order to stay alive. Many travel agencies, over time, have become order takers that execute predefined trips specified by the travelers. These travel agencies don't add much value to the individual traveler or corporation they serve other than to provide up-to-date availability and cost information. With new on-line travel reservation tools, customers can now search out different travel options and execute reservations themselves. These tools threaten to displace traditional travel agencies unless their agents are given discretion to become travel consultants who add value by advising the travelers and corporations they serve.

Innovating the Range of Discretion

If there are to be points in the process where discretion is desired, then the allowable range of that discretion must also be defined. A range of discretion must be specified because, in order to run an effective and profitable service organization, there must be some level of predictability to employee actions.

When innovating the range of discretion, the first of the two available choices is "complete customization," in which full discretion is given within a range to a person (or machine) that then creates a different outcome every time. This outcome will differ from person to person and customer to customer. For example, Disney gives its theme park employees a great amount of discretion to ensure that each guest has a memorable, enjoyable experience.

The second choice for innovating the range of discretion is mass-customization, in which there are preset options but a standard process within each option. For example, the quarterback of a professional football team is executing a mass-customized service with each passing play. As the play begins, he has the discretion to throw the ball to one of three or four other players, who are running specific, predefined routes, depending on the situation.

Often discretion is limited to managers, but any employee interacting with customers could be a candidate for helping the service process seem unique for the individual customer. Beyond people, computers and paper can be the point of discretion. For example, consider the impact of computers on the banking industry. Part of the successful introduction of ATMs into retail banking was the discretion it gave to customers by offering interaction with the bank twenty-four hours a day as well as many banking choices.

Used in concert, the three variables of process steps, points of discretion, and range of discretion are the places to focus innovation when designing service processes that deliver exceptional customer experiences. Like the knobs on the television, these variables can all be adjusted to produce an innovative and different service experience for customers. The challenge is in determining the new settings for each variable that, collectively, will produce a valuable service experience for customers.

Rules of thumb are of little help here. The answer lies in the simple fact that customers are the ones who determine the value and innovativeness of one service experience over another. How well a service fulfills their perceived need or helps them to uniquely solve an underlying problem is how customers will judge a service experience.

Therefore, creating a unique process experience means designing the service process to solve a targeted group of customers' problems through the transfer of a unique set of benefits.

Innovating Through Service Enablers

A service experience is something intangible. Producing it requires the coming together of various components like the performers and support props for a Broadway musical described earlier. These components then, or service enablers, are the means by which services are rendered or delivered. Service enablers themselves can either be tangible or intangible. In the example of home maid service, the items that enable this service to be performed include:

- cleaning supplies
- mops
- sponges
- brooms
- toilet bowl brushes
- buckets
- rags/towels
- gloves

Obviously, without these enablers, it would be nearly impossible to conduct the service and deliver the experience expected by customers.

Every service has a long list of enablers. And innovating these enablers is important and can, in fact, lead to strategic value and competitive differentiation. But there lurks a dark side to enablers. Like the trap of overstandardizing the service process, placing too much emphasis on the enablers is a trap that has taken many service organizations out of the service business and into the product business. Every service business has its enabler Achilles heel. For hotels, it is the physical building; for airlines, the plane; for consulting firms, their methodologies; for florists, their flowers; for special interest groups or associations, their agenda. In addition, the last decade has seen that computers and technology applied in most service businesses dramatically impact how services are performed.

The arrival of information technology into service businesses has been both a blessing and a curse relative to strategically designing the service process. On the positive side, technology has given businesses broader and more adaptable capabilities, and enabled service processes to be shortened or made more reliable in order to deliver new benefits to customers. But too often the technology itself is viewed as the point of differentiation.

For example, at the vortex of IRI's (Information Resources Inc.) service offering is an extremely complex and active service enabler—its database. But at times customers and employees become confused as to whether the database, and the research reports it produces, is being sold; or whether the database is an enabler of a complete service experience that focuses on the use of market information for strategic decision-making.

Another example is the typical corporate bank that tries to make its software technology the main source of innovation and differentiation. Often, the software has been created to make the operation more efficient and cost competitive. The advanced technology can give the illusion that customers will derive important benefits. When banks vigorously promote to customers that their new image technology allows them to process checks more effectively, or that their new ATM software enables faster reconciliation between accounts, they are heading for innovation wasteland. Customers don't care about the enablers in and of themselves, and will definitely not switch providers because of them. It's the benefit provided by the enabler that customers care about. This is not to suggest that a service organization should not promote their enabler innovations! Rather, the enabler innovations should be promoted as part of the overall service system and in a secondary position to the benefits being produced by the overall service concept.

Hopefully, the prior concerns about keeping enablers in their proper perspective does not cause companies to abandon the notion of using them to design innovative, effective service processes. They are an essential part of the service experience and provide much fertile ground for strategic innovation. They should also be continuously innovated and improved upon as another way to keep customers seeing and feeling increased value and uniqueness.

Innovating enablers can be thought of in two ways:

1. **Providing the desired functionality in a better way.** For example, the use of portable, attachable microphones by musical performers or seminar leaders provides the functionality of "voices being heard clearly" in a better way than handheld microphones or no microphones at all.

2. **Providing the functionality in a different way.** For example, ServiceMaster innovated its mops and the technique of mopping (side to side instead of front to back) such that the functionality of "cleanly mopped floors" is done differently than competitors and conventional approaches. The result is that customers believe their floors are cleaner and receive more professional care. This belief translates to higher perceived value for ServiceMaster.

The challenge becomes inventing, improving, and then implementing enablers that add to the benefit of the overall service. Whether the enablers are part of the experience customers see or whether they stay behind the scenes, they should be considered. For example, a hypothetical new airline service for the business traveler could have the airline focusing on new enablers that support the benefits of "your extended office" or "your flying conference center." This would require enabler innovations such as booth seating, flip-up work tables, privacy curtains, flexible food service, special reservations, and flight attendants who are business assistants instead of food servers.

Learning from Others—the Catalog Industry

The catalog industry is an example of service process innovation. This has truly been a service industry success story, as it has impressively grown from its roots as simply mail-order books for retail stores such as Sears. Today, an overabundance of niche players crowd this marketplace. Some specialize in specific types of merchandise such as clothing, food, or sound recordings; others are geared toward specific interests and lifestyles such as avid skiers. Some have even micro-niched, such as Hammacher Schlemmer as an upscale supplier of luxury items. It is hard to imagine that any more catalog niches exist; but, in fact, new catalogs continue to be launched each year.

What has separated the successful players in the catalog industry from the rest is their dedication to being service organizations first—and a product-marketing channel and provider second. For example, Lands' End and L.L. Bean distinguished their service offerings with "no questions asked" return policies; lifetime guarantees on all products; and swift, friendly, knowledgeable service. Now, however, these are standard services customers expect from all catalogers. And worse, customers are now so conditioned to these service guarantees, that they often hold off on their Christmas purchasing until the week before Christmas. This makes it more difficult to differentiate Lands' End from L.L. Bean on anything but price and merchandise selection, since both offer conservative apparel and accessories to affluent customers.

L.L. Bean has responded with a growth through diversification strategy. They have launched several secondary specialty units including Kids, Coming Home, Textures, Beyond Button Downs, and The Territory Ahead, and aggressively expanded into Europe and Japan. Lands' End, on the other hand, appears more focused on strategically innovating its core offering through a unique process experience. For example, it has introduced a new step in its delivery process, specifically a service called "Specialty Shoppers." This process innovation lets customers interact on the phone with an expert who can help coordinate outfits or plan wardrobes. In addition, Lands' End was an early entrant on the Internet for both offensive as well as defensive reasons. The Internet offers a means for customers to be on-line and more interactive in their relationships with Lands' End employees. This new channel creates all kinds of possibilities to dramatically innovate the process of buying clothing at home. For defensive reasons, Lands' End is pursuing the Internet, because the Internet has the long-term potential to completely redefine the paper-based and direct-mailed catalog industry.

The catalog industry has transformed from its beginnings as a direct marketing vehicle for retail stores into a service industry of convenience. However, there are recent signs that the industry has begun to progress back to being merely "retail stores at home," competing solely on differentiation in the products being sold. Look for leaders such as Lands' End to go counter to conventional product-thinking and re-innovate the definition of its service business and how it delivers benefits to customers.

Conclusion

The best service companies are focused on being in the *service* business. They design world-class service processes that deliver unique, valued customer experiences. Hertz, LensCrafters, Shouldice Hospital, Taco Bell, Southwest Airlines, Walt Disney Theme Parks, ServiceMaster, and Lands' End demonstrate the endless opportunities for innovating and differentiating a service through the process dimension. Some words of caution—avoid the temptation to standardize the process or mimic the competitors' processes in the name of quality or cost reduction. Like the tendency to standardize the service offerings, standardizing the service process also creates commodity service experiences that deliver ever-declining profit margins.

CHAPTER 11

Engage Your People

PEOPLE ARE THE PRIMARY SOURCE OF MARKET leadership during the delivery of services. Nowhere is this more evident than with Home Depot, the country's largest home-improvement retailer. Serving customers at Home Depot is a strategy-driven activity. Under the charge of standardization and cost savings, many companies are finding ways to take their employees *out* of the delivery equation. Home Depot is looking to its people to make a difference in the service experience of every customer. It's a culture driven by a management that believes "our employees are what makes us different from the competition"—i.e., keep them *in* the equation.

Home Depot's philosophy, like some other service organizations that are strategically engaging their people, goes beyond mere employee empowerment. It has instilled in its people a "passion" to serve customers. This starts with employee recruiting criteria that emphasize interpersonal skills and policies that facilitate personal interest in interacting with people. But this passion is inflamed by allowing employees to be themselves and to use their natural talents and instincts when interacting with customers. Home Depot is open and trusting with the notion that its employees will do what is best for the customer. It will support its employees in the decisions they need to make to ensure the customer's satisfaction.

The challenge for service market leaders is to assure that the customer experience is truly an experience—a feeling. And it is a feeling unique unto each customer. To develop powerful market-dominating people strategies, the customer's perspective must be sought out and then made to permeate the psyche of every employee. To illustrate the message of this chapter, the following story is about Linda, a fictional Home Depot customer, and her unique shopping experience.

A Customer's Experience

As Linda left her local hardware store, she didn't feel very good. "Why was it that no one seemed to have the time to really help me?" she wondered. Her feeling was compounded by a romanticized memory of yesteryear when a trip to the hardware store with her father meant spending lots of time learning about new things and talking and laughing with people at the store. "It's not as though I couldn't find anyone or they wouldn't answer my questions. But it was more the way they answered them," she mused. "They gave me short and courteous answers accompanied by a pointing finger showing me the way. Maybe they are trained to be so efficient that they aren't allowed to spend any more than ten seconds answering my questions!" she thought as she drove away. Linda still had to find a solution to her leaking shower stall and door problem.

Linda gasped as she entered Home Depot's gigantic store. The idea of everything under one roof is a scary reality to the average customer walking into the building. "Oh great," Linda thought. "How will I ever figure out what to do in this apparently 'self-help' store?" She began doing the "police-line walk"—head back, eyes glazed over, trying to read the fifteen-foot-high aisle signs.

But then Raoul appeared. With a shiny employee badge and a smile on his face, he asked, "Are you by chance the ceiling inspector we heard was coming today?" Linda looked at him, startled for a moment, and then began to laugh. "No, just one of the lost sheep here," she retorted. "I see. Are you a kitchen or bathroom lost sheep?" he asked. "Definitely a bathroom type," she replied. "Great!" Raoul exclaimed, "That's where I'm headed. Let's go together."

As they walked through the store, the friendly and casual conversation continued. Raoul found out that Linda's shower door was cracked and the base tub leaked. He reassured her that it was not a big problem and that she would probably be able to fix it herself. When they got to the right section, Raoul brought over someone who seemed to be a shower door expert. He listened to Raoul describe Linda's problem and then suggested which products to buy. To Linda's surprise, they were not the most expensive doors on the shelves, and he suggested caulking the tub instead of replacing it. At this point, she couldn't stand it anymore. It had gone way beyond just good customer service. Puzzled, she asked, "Okay, what gives? Was I the 100th customer in the door or something? I mean, what a gimmick, asking me all kinds of questions, and then recommending the least expensive solution. Are you guys in training and being watched by your manager?"

Raoul chuckled. "Actually, Linda, I am one of the managers. Quite honestly, we just enjoy getting to know you. It makes us feel good to know we were able to help. Our only hope is that you'll come back again and say 'hello.'" Linda smiled. "Very impressive—and innovative. Am I coming back? You bet!"

As Linda walked to her car, she felt elated. She had a solution to her problem, she had learned how to do the repairs herself, and she felt as though someone personally cared about her. The Home Depot store seemed much warmer and friendlier than even her local hardware store.

Raoul headed off to his 3:00 P.M. meeting to close the employee orientation session going on in the meeting room. He stood in the middle of the room where he could look squarely into the eyes of his newest employees. After a brief period of absolute silence, he sincerely stated, "Customer service is in the eye of the beholder. Many companies give it lip service, but we literally *define* customer service *as taking care of the customer. And we do. We want to not only meet but exceed each customer's expectations. Each and every one of you in this room is what makes us different from the competition." And with that he smiled and said, "Welcome to the team!"*

Getting People—Employees and Customers—Engaged

Engaging the people component of service delivery can produce a market-dominating impact. It is not about making people more creative. It is not about increasing the quality of delivery execution. Certainly, these are vital areas. But the final, powerful component of a service market leader is the way service people are involved and how they act during delivery. It is about customers feeling that a unique and differentiated service experience is unfolding for them, personally.

Suppose you are in the hospital for tests and your doctor makes a point of stopping by your room. After asking, "How are you doing?" and learning that you are concerned about how to explain to your spouse the complex results, she immediately walks to the phone and makes the phone call for you. Now how do you feel? Pretty special and valued!

The Need for People Innovation

For most service organizations, the strategy of delivery has been to make the process routine and to take variability out. Under the banner of standardization, service delivery tactics have required more and more automation and electronic relationships. The mind-set of "We can't afford to use our expensive delivery system and high level of people involvement for all customers" exists across many service companies. These companies believe they need to "improve profitability and efficiency by eliminating wasteful and error-producing activities by our people." Some even go so far as to say "In our business, we need to give the people interfacing with customers a simple-to-follow process with detailed instructions, lots of 'how-to' training, and threats backed up with action if they don't follow the instructions exactly." The debilitating assumption by management is that employees can't be trusted and that management should standardize, control, and monitor employee activities to ensure quality. This attitude, of course, is the antithesis of people innovation.

Many years ago, there was a national survey conducted among college students to determine their favorite television show. Researchers were not surprised that the enormously successful new shows *60 Minutes*, *M*A*S*H*, and *Saturday Night Live* were among the top vote getters. What did shock them, however, was that the number-one ranked show was the Bugs Bunny cartoon. The survey showed that college students identified with Bugs' ability to use his creativity and resourcefulness to outsmart his adversaries. Service employees involved with the delivery of services will have to use their ingenuity and skills as well.

One might ask "Aren't you just talking about good customer service and giving employees empowerment?" The answer is "No and no." First of all, most service managers—and business people in general—quickly lump any mention of good customer service or empowerment management into the cost-saving stereotype. This stereotype might as well be referred to as "Getting the humans to do it the right way—answer the phones better, respond to questions better, execute the process more uniformly, or train managers to motivate the humans better." We use the phrase "the humans" because we could just as easily substitute "the primates" or "the canines" or any other trainable species that responds to rules, instructions, and motivation techniques. Second, good customer service and employee empowerment are concepts that peaked in popularity in the late 1980s. Service managers have become a bit callused to the topic. The prevailing view is that "We've been there, done that." Third, for many service companies, the pendulum for operational excellence has swung too far—usually under the banner of "Quality is Rule One." Yes, a service organization must deliver consistently high-quality experiences to be competitive. And, yes, service companies have invested heavily in information technology to accomplish their quality goals. But all too often, these investments in operations and infrastructure end up driving the strategies of the organization. It's like the tail wagging the dog.

Too much focus on quality and technology threatens to transform service companies into product companies. Major banks today represent the epitome of this example. Acquisition is the growth strategy of the day and bigness is the leadership goal. In order to make acquisitions and bigness work on the inside, huge investments in new systems and systems integration are required. This results in tremendous operational capabilities. But then the mistake happens, and it is very subtle and rarely noticed even among marketing and sales management. Managers assume new technology and operating capabilities are really the same thing as new services. They think it is merely an exercise in packaging, communicating, and distributing these new capabilities to customers. Customers always respond to internal technology investments with genuine self-interest, "So what's in it for me beyond a lower price, since you'll be the one seeing lots of cost savings?"

Delivering Individualized Experiences

The market leadership goal for the delivery of services should be to produce individualized experiences for each customer. While this cannot happen one hundred percent of the time, the closer to this goal an organization comes, the greater will be the perception of uniqueness and value-added among customers. And these satisfied customers reward service providers with more sales at better prices.

The idea of individualized experiences, however, terrifies most managers in service organizations. Conventional wisdom states that achieving scale and mass distribution is the way to profitability. For years, insurance companies have followed this thinking. They seem to have mixed up the roles of delivery and sales. In the past, insurance agents were trusted advisers who first understood each customer's unique requirements and then sifted through the maze of insurance offerings to piece together the right insurance policy or solution for them. If a customer needed to make a claim against a policy, the agent once again took a personal role in making sure the customer was taken care of and personally satisfied. Thus, the individualized service experience consisted of interactions before and after purchasing a policy and involved a person with whom the customer had a close relationship throughout the entire experience. Insurance agents were involved both in sales and service experience delivery. In those days, it was a powerful, differentiating, and profitable offering that combined new insurance products, innovations in the process of working with the insurance company, and a relationship with an agent who made it all work uniquely for each customer.

But then the notion of industrializing services came into full swing. Easy cost savings were realized by achieving scale economies in operations. These economies necessitated standardized insurance products that did not require alterations. Today, most insurance agents have become purely salespeople for a commodity insurance product that is sequentially produced, mass distributed, and then serviced as needed. The service experience, in reality, is dormant until something bad happens to a customer's body or possession. And only a handful of insurance companies recognize that this is their moment of service-experience truth in which they have the opportunity to deliver an individualized experience. Usually, however, it becomes an impersonal claims process driven by the desire to standardize and neuter the personality of the people delivering it. And then the industry laments the decrease of loyalty and increase in price sensitivity among consumers. This is why innovative market leaders, such as Progressive Insurance, who have included the people component in creating differentiating and value-adding offerings, are finding profitable growth an attainable objective.

Individual Creativity and Proactiveness

At the heart of delivering individualized experiences are the hearts of individual employees. They desire to turn on their personalities and creativities, to leverage technology and other resources, and to give customers a unique experience. During the last fifty years, there have been four distinct phases in the evolution of companies' views toward employees who interact with customers (see Figure 11.1, page 184). It began with companies fulfilling the basic security need of working Americans by providing "employment"—the lifelong job in most cases. Next came a phase in which managers learned about the discipline of employee motivation and provided "encouragement."

Figure 11.1 **Phases of a Company's View Toward Its People**

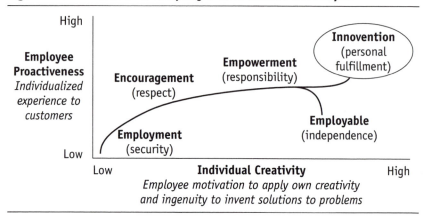

The third phase evolved into the "empowerment" of employees so that they felt more responsible, because they could react to customer situations and make decisions before checking with a supervisor. These three phases resulted in a positive progression toward more and more enlightened approaches to addressing the nonmonetary, intrinsic motivators of employees.

But since the late 1980s, a troublesome new phase has been gaining momentum. Coming on the heels of reengineering and downsizing, human resources departments are professing a new religion of enlightenment—"employable." This latest movement toward being "employable" looks good on the surface: "develop the skills of our people to make them easily employable should they decide (or be asked) to leave the company." It appears to be the accomplishment of a decade-long pursuit to have employees become more independent and entrepreneurial.

In reality, however, "employable" is just a more pleasant way of saying "layoff-ready employees." This reality has a potentially negative effect—a downward spiral as employees feel abandoned and then become disconnected from the values and purpose of the organization. Similarly, companies feel a lack of responsibility toward downsizings and layoffs because they have "given layoff victims better skills to take elsewhere." The net effect on service employees, charged with delivering outstanding service is a reversion back to worrying about job security. The stress of worrying about job security dramatically shuts down the personal ingenuity and personality of employees when they are interacting with customers.

The strategic market leadership of service companies must also include delivering an individualized experience to customers. The four phases previously mentioned do not accomplish this. While empowerment is certainly the closest, it is essentially reactive in nature. Likewise, good customer service most often has employees focused on being responsive. It is a philosophy that tells the customer "Ask and we will jump through hoops to respond." During delivery, this gives customers the feeling of being pampered or receiving quality care. But it also leaves customers feeling as though they have been involved in some sort of mass distribution of goods.

For example, the employees of the large retailer in Chicago Marshall Field's are well known for their responsive service. The company spends considerable time and effort training and motivating employees to look attentive, to smile, to cheerfully answer questions and to make themselves available to customers. Unfortunately, "reactive" and "responsive" do not give customers the feeling of a unique, memorable experience. Responsive employees are, in effect, product representatives who facilitate your product buying experience. They are part of mass distribution, not the delivery of a service experience.

Now contrast Marshall Field's with Nordstrom, a retailer devoted to being a service organization that delivers individual experiences. Nordstrom customers describe their experience with comments such as "fun," "energizing," "educating," "fulfilling," "I got exactly what I needed," and "the woman I worked with did all the running around." These descriptors come from people who have had a service experience tailored for them. Nordstrom has created a delivery approach that has their employees at the center of the action. These employees are not clerks waiting to process an order. For example, in women's clothes they use individual dressing areas, free on-site tailors, a full line of fashionable clothing, and their own clothing expertise as components of an individual experience they creatively and genuinely weave uniquely for each woman. This is what gives these customers a feeling that Nordstrom provides an innovative service.

"Innovention"

To complement the market leadership elements of concept innovation and process innovation introduced in previous chapters, leading service companies are pursuing a people leadership strategy called "innovention." It is the *proactive intervention* by employees with customers to create an individualized service experience. It requires that management provide the right leadership; create the appropriate work environment; and provide support, tools, skills, and rewards that propel employees to be proactive with customers. Innovention is the collective energy of every person involved in delivering a service to make the experience specific and unique for each and every customer. It is a passion for engaging with customers and performing for them.

Flight attendants for Southwest Airlines enthusiastically and theatrically give the obligatory safety preamble that explains how to buckle a seat belt and where to store bags. The airline broke the historic and boring industry practice of having stoic flight attendants be disengaged from customers. Instead of the traditional job of safety-agents-in-waiting and food servers, flight attendants on Southwest are entertainers proactively making sure passengers have a good time while flying. Passengers on the plane experience a performance that comes across as something unique just for that flight, because the flight attendants have been able to share their personalities and genuine interest in each passenger. Other airlines are still mired in having their people carry out routine tasks designed as part of the mass distribution of a product called airline transportation.

But what does it take to deliver individualized experiences? Successful service leaders find the right balance among the essential delivery components of people for effectiveness, technology for efficiency, and standardization for quality. Our primary interest here is with the first component—people. To strategically innovate a service, pursuing people innovation is the key ingredient. There are four principles that must be adhered to in order to maximize a people innovation impact:

1. Put people back into the equation as the core part of creating uniqueness in the delivery of a service.
2. Create a system that allows people to rapidly create tailored solutions for specific customers.

3. Give people the skills that will enable them to provide customers with an individualized experience.
4. Pursue integrated targeted customer relationships where individuals from the provider and customer organizations have ongoing personal relationships.

Put People Back in the Delivery Equation

Putting people back in the delivery equation starts with having employees become a larger factor (preferably the largest) in how services get delivered. As organizations develop a myriad of processes for the delivery of their service, they must remember to emphasize the power and creativity of their people. For it is in the initial development stages of these processes that the actual performers of the service can contribute their individual and creative skills—in essence, bring passion to their personal delivery of that service. It is vital that employees be allowed to leverage their own intellect and have a degree of discretion or personal judgment when interacting with their customers.

Forget the idea that technology should always replace people. Used intelligently, technology should support or enable the efforts of people. When technology is the only delivery format, then a service organization becomes nothing more than a software business.

Enable Employees to Create Tailored Solutions

To practically create tailored solutions, organizations need to place customers into potential "experience-desired" categories and then to challenge employees to meet customer expectations. An Innovention philosophy and a people-innovation approach contribute to an employee's ability to do this. For example, let's say that for a four-hour flight, a flight attendant has ten people to serve in first class. Some of the business people want to be pampered (the "relaxers"), while other business people want to be able to work (the "workers"). Still a third group wants to be able to interact with their colleague (the "talkers"). The attendant should be able to alter what she or he does to address these specific experience expectations. For the worker, the attendant may have to consider all of the following possibilities, depending on the circumstances he or she perceives: providing quick food service or no food at all; offer to attach a different type of table or flexible desk lamp; or change the seat of the worker if the person next to them is not working, to provide for quieter, uninterrupted time. The point is that the service delivery process should allow for the attendant's critical thinking and creative action.

Whether dealing with consumers or business-to-business customers, the key is having employees modify their behavior based on the unique, individual needs of each customer. The old automobile service stations died out because they competed on speed and convenience, not on individualized service. But nowadays, people say the pace of life is too fast and "I'll pump my own gas if I can save five cents per gallon!" In reality, this represents less than $50 per year for the average driver. But things have changed. Before, people didn't want to get out of their cars. Now, with convenience stores inside, gas station attendants should be encouraging customers to get out of their cars and into the store, where they can linger and buy all kinds of high-margin items. Why not take their car through the car wash for them, provide free fluid and air check, or a windshield wash? (Do these things sound familiar from days gone by?)

In another example, express-mail delivery drivers often have lots of checklists. They must execute sequential and repeating patterns—sometimes to the insane level of "Now turn off the ignition key" or "Before leaving the vehicle, check to be sure all doors are shut." However, when a driver lingers long enough to inquire about the special tracking needs of a new shipping manager, customer loyalty increases.

Provide the Necessary Skills

The third principle of people innovation involves giving employees the skills that will enable them to give customers an individualized experience. Obviously, the organization must first have the right people (see Chapter 12). Service leaders uniformly spend more time and expend more effort selecting and hiring the best people than do other organizations. These leaders are disciplined to hire only when an outstanding candidate surfaces and not because a quota of new hires must be met. Similarly, leading people-innovation companies require early recognition of a "bad hire" and take quick action to address the situation.

With the right selections, building the skills of people performing the service is straightforward. This second requirement is driven by the definition of a strategic premise: what specific expertise does an employee need to have? Skill building is an integrated orchestration of (1) setting plans for employees to gain the necessary expertise, (2) providing mentoring and quality leadership, and (3) motivating employees to take action through rewards and incentives.

Develop Integrated Customer Relationships

It's fine to compete just on the service concept and service process experience, but this can still leave a competitive weapon dormant. Quick oil change outlets such as Jiffy Lube serve as an example. In the early days of this new industry, the concept of a ten-minute oil-and-filter change, wrapped in a reliable process that required no reservations, allowed many competitors to flourish. But it has also produced a commodity perception by customers toward the various providers of this service. What some providers like Jiffy Lube and Midas Mufflers have done is to bring their employees, as well as customers, more into the delivery equation, creating tailored solutions and individualized customer experiences. They have done this by: encouraging customers to talk directly with the mechanic who will work on the car; having the mechanic further discuss the car's needs once a quick diagnosis has been completed; and enabling customers to watch the work being done behind a glass-enclosed waiting room. This, by design, increases the time spent by employees interacting with customers, which also gives more opportunity for individualized service delivery.

Conclusion

Much has been written about the direct link between employee satisfaction, employee retention, employee productivity, and service quality—as well as the corresponding linkage to customer satisfaction, loyalty, and profitability. The factors influencing employee satisfaction and retention are complex and varied, including effective selection, job design, training, career opportunities, compensation, recognition, supporting technology, teamwork, and culture. Because of the wealth of information already on this topic, this book doesn't intend to reiterate it. Rather, companies must realize that the drive to standardize service operations and reduce employee discretion—all in the name of quality—has removed a competitive weapon from many service companies. They need to put people back into the equation as innovation engines for delivering unique, valued service experiences.

With the advent of micromarketing and mass-customization, product and service companies alike must provide customers with individualized experiences. One of the challenges is to build flexibility and customizable capabilities into the operations themselves. Another challenge is to build service delivery systems around employees who are directly involved with customers. Promoting individual creativity and proactiveness (Innovention) is what service leaders pursue with cultural passion. When people innovation approaches are combined with the other strategies of market leadership, an organization is well on its way to providing unique and meaningful value to their customers. Activating *all* the leadership strategies is the way to invent dramatic growth, year after year.

PART IV

Keeping Ahead
of the Market

CHAPTER 12

Sustain Service Market Leadership

SERVICE MARKET LEADERS KNOW THEY CANNOT be content with the status quo. Market boundaries shift, new competitors enter, new services are launched; all at a chilling pace. Guaranteed. What are the secrets to sustaining market leadership over time?

Service companies might learn some lessons from Willow Creek Community Church, located in South Barrington, Illinois. Willow Creek has sustained an impressive track record. After only twenty-three years of "being in business," it is now the largest church in North America. It also actively supports more than three thousand churches worldwide through the Willow Creek Association.

In the late 1970s, Willow Creek was merely a few high school and college students, passionately committed to their beliefs, who wanted to do church differently. At the time, they met in an old theater. As the church was starting up, the founders went door to door to find out the reasons why people had stopped attending church. They found that people with no interest in church gave consistent answers:

"It's not relevant to my life."
"The services are boring and predictable."
"People are always asking me for money."

"The pastor makes me feel guilty, so I leave feeling worse than when I came."

The founders of Willow Creek focused their attention on addressing these issues. They felt church could and should be different. It should be relevant. It should be interesting. And it should be actively involved in the process of life change. So they designed the organization and its services to meet the needs of these "unchurched" people and to give people a reason to invite other friends and family.

Willow Creek has developed two different church services designed for the needs of different audiences. The weekend services target "seekers" and are designed to expose people to the Christian faith in a relevant, nonthreatening way. These "seeker" services include updated music, drama, and messages on relevant life topics such as relationships, parenting, financial management, and work. The midweek services are designed for "believers," people who have made a commitment to the Christian faith and are looking to deepen their spiritual growth within a community of other believers. These "believer" services provide an opportunity for singing, worship, and additional in-depth teaching. Willow Creek now offers four "seeker" weekend services and has an average weekend attendance of more than fifteen thousand people, and it offers two midweek "believer services." They moved out of the theater long ago and purchased their own facility, and have now expanded the facility several times. How have they sustained a leadership position?

First, Willow Creek continues to expand the breadth and depth of their services to address a wide variety of needs—offering services and ministry opportunities for people of different ages, married and single people, families, people at different stages of spiritual development, and people with various life challenges. As their membership has grown and members' needs have changed, Willow Creek has continuously developed new programs to address these needs. They foster an entrepreneurial environment conducive to continuous innovation.

Second, Willow Creek pays incredible attention to its hiring process. How can a church attract and retain talented people when they offer less than market wages? To begin with, their clear and compelling mission attracts people who want to help realize that mission. Willow Creek then explores each individual's unique talents, gifts, and preferences, and works hard to align each person's role in such a way that it maximizes their unique abilities. The leaders lead; the teachers teach; the administrators administrate.

Third, Willow Creek has a passionate commitment to leadership development. The challenge with many churches is that they are inextricably linked to their senior pastor. As the senior pastor goes, so goes the church. Willow Creek knows the church must be sustainable beyond its founder, Bill Hybels. They focus on hiring and developing leaders for the next generation, not only for their own church but for other churches as well. For example, church leaders from around the world gather twice a year to attend Willow Creek's Church Leadership Conference. Here they learn some of the leadership successes and challenges from Willow Creek's history and how to apply these lessons to their own situations. Every summer Willow Creek also arranges and hosts a Leadership Summit where they bring in the best leadership talent they can find—including leaders from business and academia—to teach on the topic of leadership.

Finally, Willow Creek is planning for the future. They have put in place a long-term planning process to help the church survive and thrive in the future. In fact, Willow Creek is in the process of reinventing themselves to ensure they are relevant to the next generation. A few years ago, the church added a weekend service designed for the unique needs and preferences of "Generation X'ers."

More impressive than its size is Willow Creek's consistency. Yes, there have been bumps along the way. But the church has stayed true to its mission while continuing to increase its impact on the lives of attendees, the community, and churches around the world. They have put in place the mechanisms to sustain leadership over the long run—including continuous organization learning, innovation, leadership development, and growth. This chapter addresses the processes for sustaining market leadership.

Sustaining Market-Driven Behavior

Service market leaders sustain their leadership by institutionalizing market-driven behavior. What does market-driven behavior look like? It represents a shift from an inward focus on service offerings and operations to an outward focus on customers and their needs, competitors, and market shifts. To sustain market-driven behavior requires putting processes in place that help a company continuously and systematically:

- understand who customers are and determine which ones to target
- uncover what customers need and deliver on those needs
- understand why customers buy and what motivates their loyalty
- understand how customers want to buy (e.g., preferred channels of access) and provide those channels
- know competitors and determine where to be different

A lot of activities within a service company can contribute to accomplishing these worthy objectives. But achieving systematic and sustainable market-driven behavior, over the long run, requires service companies to institute five business processes:

1. Market Requirements Process: uncovering customer needs and competitor activities, and disseminating information throughout the organization
2. New Service Development Process: developing and launching market-driven innovations
3. People Adoption Process: selecting and retaining the right people.
4. Leadership Development Process: developing the next generation of externally focused leaders
5. Long-Term Planning Process: charting the course toward future opportunities

Clearly, these are not the only business processes required for ongoing success. We've focused on these five processes because they are at the heart of keeping an organization focused externally and using the insights learned to create unique value for customers—on an ongoing, systematic basis. That is how service market leaders sustain their leadership.

Market Requirements Process

The market requirements process is all about collecting, analyzing, and initiating responses to the requirements of customers, as well as competitor activities. Market requirements guide overall company direction, as well as service- and market-specific decisions. The market requirements process feeds the long-term planning process, and must be executed on a continuous basis throughout the year.

In most service organizations, one functional group (e.g., market research) serves as a single point of contact for capturing and consolidating market requirements in a consistent way. Beyond collecting market information, the challenge facing most companies is disseminating the information to appropriate audiences within the company in a timely way:

- service offering–specific requirements to service managers
- market-specific requirements to market managers
- customer service requirements to the customer service organization
- new market and service requirements to the business development function and new service developers
- selling requirements to the sales function
- communication requirements to the marketing communications function

Figure 12.1 (page 198) depicts the process at a high level.

In too many service companies we have seen the market requirements process narrowly defined as a customer satisfaction measurement process. Too many service companies are obsessed with measuring customer satisfaction. An example would be the bank that tracked more than five hundred measures on a weekly basis, mentioned earlier in this book. They had more information than they could possibly act on.

Companies focused on customer satisfaction measurement can identify changes in key measures, quickly correct problems, and reward superior performance. Of course, comparisons of customer satisfaction measures over time can be insightful and useful. Customer satisfaction measurement, however, is only one component of the market requirements process. Customer satisfaction is, by definition, a measurement of the past—past customer needs and past company performance. In addition, customer satisfaction measurements report on things that are easily articulated by customers. This type of information is helpful for incremental improvements in service quality,

Figure 12.1 **Market Requirements Process**

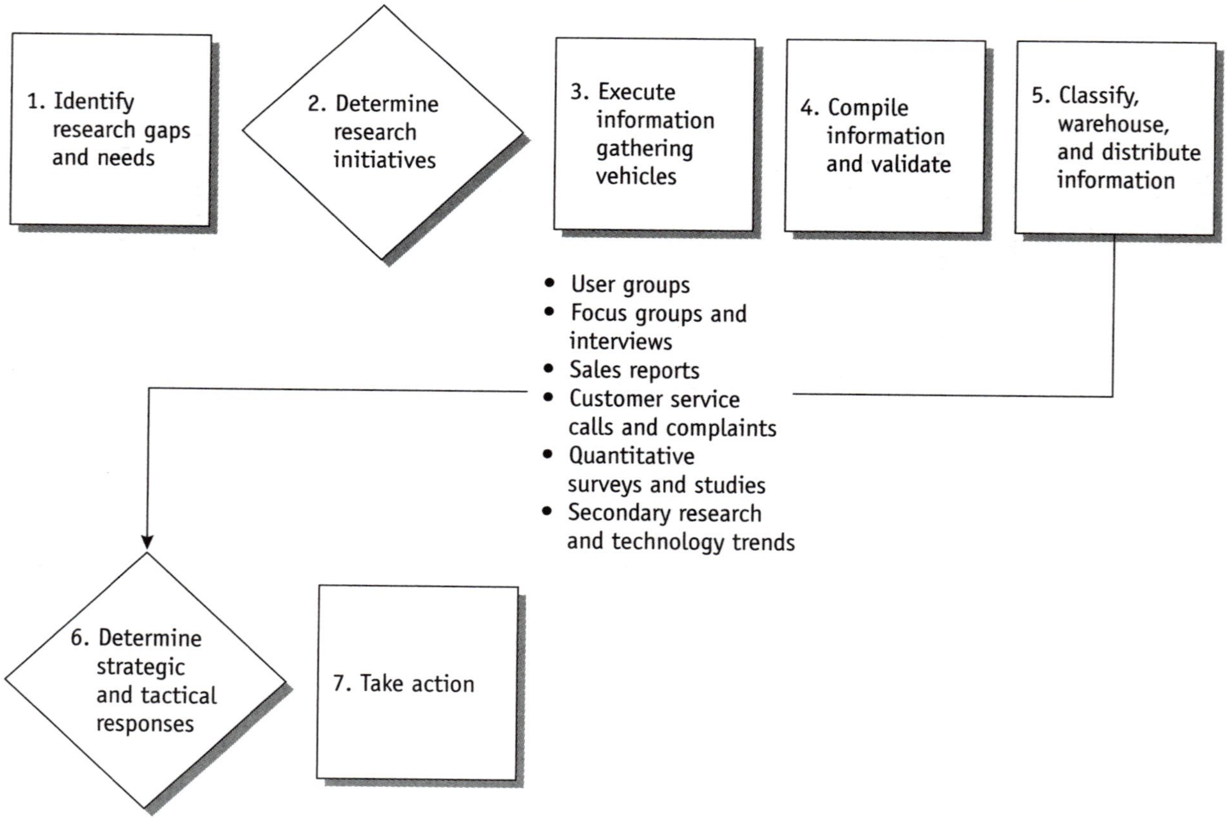

1. Identify research gaps and needs

2. Determine research initiatives

3. Execute information gathering vehicles

- User groups
- Focus groups and interviews
- Sales reports
- Customer service calls and complaints
- Quantitative surveys and studies
- Secondary research and technology trends

4. Compile information and validate

5. Classify, warehouse, and distribute information

6. Determine strategic and tactical responses

7. Take action

delivery, operations, and service features. However, customer satisfaction research is not particularly useful for innovation and growth.

What customer satisfaction measures tend to miss are the future opportunities; they don't uncover unmet needs, underserved segments of customers, shifts in value, or the real reasons why customers switch providers. These issues are difficult for customers to articulate, and nearly impossible to uncover through quantitative customer satisfaction research. In fact, service companies are just starting to wake up to the fact that satisfied customers are leaving them. Satisfaction does not guarantee loyalty.

Service companies need to ensure their market requirements process contains a healthy dose of forward-looking research that uncovers answers to questions like:

- What are customers' unmet needs? Which of these are most intense and most pervasive?
- What macro trends are impacting our customers' lives? How do these trends relate to our services?
- What new technologies could be applied to address customers' most intense needs?
- What are customers doing outside of their service experience with us? What opportunities exist to address related problems or needs that we don't directly address today?
- How do customers perceive our brand? Competitors' brands?
- Which segments of customers are growing? Which segments are underserved by current offerings?
- Who are the most loyal customers? Why do they stay? Why do others defect? Are the defectors worth keeping? What might cause them to stay?

The answers to these questions go beyond correcting today's problems. They can shed light on future growth opportunities.

New Service Development Process

Having a formal new service development process should be self-evident. Right? Yet more than one-half of the new service developers responding to a recent study indicated that their organizations don't follow a formal process (Kuczmarski & Assoc. 1995). This compares to a much smaller percentage of respondents from product companies. Perhaps many service companies have not adopted a rigorous new service development process due to the intangible nature of services or the lack of competition in certain regulated service industries.

The primary benefits of implementing a formalized new service development process are as follows:

- improved new service introduction success rates
- reduced development cycle time
- improved organization communications and enhanced training through use of a common language
- increased overall return on innovation investments

Figure 12.2 (page 201) outlines a ten-step new service development process that can be customized for different service industries.

The first difference between Figure 12.2 and the processes found in most service companies is Step 1—problem identification. Few companies start their new service development efforts *in the market*. Rather, they gather a group of managers off site, hire an idea-generation facilitator, and spend a day brainstorming ideas. Other than having some fun, what they end up with at the end of the day are flip-chart-covered walls containing hundreds of ideas. But how do they sift through the ideas and find the gems? The basic problem with this approach is that company managers are not the customers. In very few instances do the managers of service companies look like or behave like their typical customer, let alone have similar needs.

The recommended ten-step approach starts with input from the market requirements process. The goal is to determine the most intense, most pervasive customer problems. What really gripes customers? What are their frustrations, complaints, concerns, and wishes? New services that are strongly grounded in an intense customer problem have a higher likelihood of success. In fact, lack of a customer need is still the number-one reason for new service failure (Kuczmarski & Assoc. 1995).

A second key difference between this ten-step process and what is found in most service companies is the ongoing need for customer involvement. Not only should customers be involved up front in sharing their problems, they should be involved throughout the process. Specifically, customers should provide ongoing input to help shape

Figure 12.2 New Service Development Process

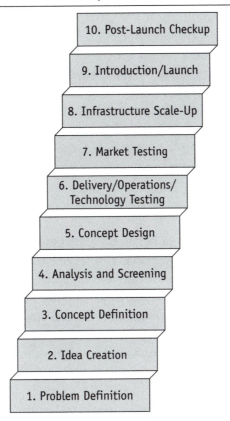

10. Post-Launch Checkup

9. Introduction/Launch

8. Infrastructure Scale-Up

7. Market Testing

6. Delivery/Operations/Technology Testing

5. Concept Design

4. Analysis and Screening

3. Concept Definition

2. Idea Creation

1. Problem Definition

and refine new service concepts. In some business-to-business industries, companies establish a customer user group to assist in the new service development process. This group of current customers is assembled on multiple occasions to offer input on their requirements, generate ideas, react to concepts, and eventually pilot new services. The risk, of course, is that the group assembled does not represent the needs of a broader market. The benefits, however, are compelling—namely, a ready group of committed, early adopters prepared to pilot the new service and help refine it.

A third key characteristic of this ten-step process is found in Steps 6–8—operational testing and scale-up. Developing new services can be more complex than new products. Services often require new delivery systems, changes in billing systems, in-depth training for customer-contact and customer service personnel, and changes in other operating functions and infrastructure; all this in addition to creating the new service offering itself. As a result, too much demand for a new service can kill it. If the delivery system is not sufficiently capable of handling demand for a new service, the entire system breaks down. Quality and consistency suffer, customers leave disappointed, and reestablishing trust may be difficult. Small-scale operational testing, in conjunction with awareness-building techniques that try to match supply and demand, are critical for ensuring the company is truly prepared to deliver a new service.

People Adoption Process

Time and again, CEOs publicly state "People are our number-one asset." And rightfully so, especially in service companies. But getting the right people makes all the difference.

One consistent theme emerges from studying service companies who have sustained market leadership over a long period of time—they have an extremely disciplined approach to selecting new employees. Specifically, these companies seem to have a template or profile describing the ideal candidate for each position. They diligently screen in candidates who fit the profile. Rather than a recruiting process, they view hiring as an "adoption" process. They work hard to select candidates whose talents, personalities, and professional goals closely fit the profiles.

In these companies, significant time and energy is invested up front in order to minimize poor hiring decisions. Cross-functional teams typically perform the recruiting in order to offer multiple perspectives on a candidate. Some companies even include customers in the recruiting process. After all, who can better represent a customer's viewpoint than an actual customer? Finally, these companies put in place an early warning evaluation system so they can quickly identify and address incorrect hiring decisions.

Having a profile is a good start. But the power of effective people selection comes from having a profile that tightly links to the company's strategic point of difference (see Chapter 6). The goal is to hire employees who are uniquely qualified to deliver on the company's point of difference. The tighter the fit between the employee profile and the company's positioning, the greater the company's ability to create a unique competitive advantage that customers value. Over time, the company builds up a workforce that truly cannot be replicated. Herb Kelleher of Southwest Airlines said it best, regarding the key contributor to success in his company:

> *Maybe someone could equal the cost. Possibly they could. Maybe someone could equal the quality of service. Possibly they could. One thing they (competitors) would find it impossible to equal, very easily at least, is the spirit of our people and the attitude that they manifest towards our customers* (Heskett, Sasser, and Schlesinger 1993).

Recall the Shouldice Hospital example from Chapter 10. Shouldice performs only one procedure—hernia operations. Think about the characteristics of doctors who fit their profile. Shouldice doesn't attract doctors who seek notoriety, upward career mobility, great wealth, or significant variety in their cases. However, Shouldice does offer a predictable work environment with reasonable hours, since they preschedule all appointments and do not have to attend to emergencies. Doctors can specialize, earn a good living, help patients, but also have a life outside of work. Weekend and evening hours are limited, and stress is relatively low. Shouldice's doctor profile had to match their business model.

One of the stated difficulties Euro Disney encountered in the early days was a poor employee fit relative to Disney's proven business model. In preparation for its opening, Euro Disney rushed to hire over eleven thousand employees in a matter of months. As a result, many of the employees hired did not fit with the Disney culture or appreciate the strict employment standards of Disney. It resulted in difficulty in maintaining Disney's historical customer service levels, as well as in excessive employee turnover.

Although recruiting time and costs for each applicant can be higher and recruiting cycles longer, successfully attracting the right people for a company's unique positioning has several benefits:

- reduced employee turnover and higher employee retention (therefore, lower long-term recruiting costs)

- reduced training costs and increased productivity
- increased employee satisfaction (which has a direct positive impact on customer satisfaction)
- increased ability to replicate the business model in multiple locations

One important implication of creating a tight link between employee selection and company positioning is the potential restriction of certain growth alternatives. Companies with a tight employee-positioning link must actively consider the fit of each growth alternative with their current people model. For example, what if Shouldice Hospital wanted to increase capacity by extending weekday and weekend business hours? This goal would conflict with the type of people they have attracted. Shouldice's implicit promise of regular work hours would be broken. Their entire model for success could be jeopardized.

Leadership Development Process

The newly hired CEO of a major technology company was charged with reversing several years of poor company performance. He spent his first few months meeting extensively with current and former customers and with a cross section of employees. In the process, he believed he uncovered one of the primary problems: his management team was sorely out of touch with customers. The new CEO was convinced his company had become too internally focused. Fresh from his own customer visits, he asked each of the company's top fifty leaders to meet with several customers and write a report on their findings. Unfortunately, rather than meeting with customers themselves, almost one-half of these leaders assigned the responsibility to one of their subordinates. Most of these leaders are no longer with the company!

Too often, service company leaders become internally focused and lose touch with their customers. As the company grows, issues related to operations, people, geographic expansion, facilities, and finances can consume management's time and attention. Operations and finance issues are important, but if leaders aren't directly serving customers or the frontline employees who serve customers, what value are they really adding?

Walk into a service company that has sustained market leadership and you will feel something very different. These organizations demonstrate three tangible actions:

1. At all levels of the organization, leaders and managers regularly spend time with customers and frontline employees. We will discuss this more in Chapter 13.
2. Leaders focus on and are obsessed with outmaneuvering the competition. This external mind-set and competitive drive is apparent and ingrained in all levels of leaders.
3. Leaders develop the next generation of leaders through formal or informal mentoring and training. These "apprentice leaders" are raised up learning the values of the company and focusing on customers and competition. One charismatic leader cannot sustain an organization's leadership position forever. A process must be in place to develop future leaders.

A start-up division within one Regional Bell Operating Company (RBOC) made a radical decision to hire a chief information officer (CIO) with a background in marketing and customer service. Not necessarily a recipe for success. Wouldn't you expect a CIO to have in-depth technical expertise? This CIO doesn't. Although she has previously worked for several high-technology companies, her biggest strength is her focus on customers and their needs—internal and external customers. She's also a great team builder and developer of emerging leaders. This CIO is a living testimony that leaders from all functions of service organizations need to be intimately involved with customers and frontline employees.

Long-Term Planning Process

The long-term planning process (sometimes called the market planning process) is critical for determining the importance of, strategies for, and resource commitment to key growth alternatives. The primary objectives of the long-term planning process are:

- to determine company strategy and competitive positioning
- to develop strategies for pursuing each market

Figure 12.3 **Long-Term Planning Process**

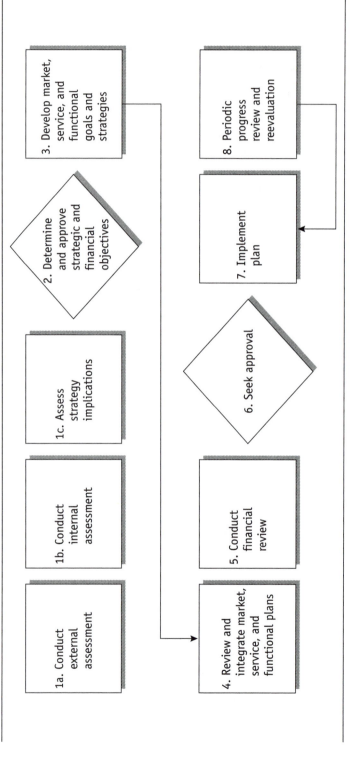

- to prioritize growth opportunities
- to allocate company resources

Figure 12.3 (page 206) outlines a high-level overview of the long-term planning process.

The long-term planning process is a discipline that ensures a company is constantly seeking out new opportunities and uncovering threats to its current business—and acting on this information in a systematic way. How did Charles Schwab first discover and create the discount brokerage market opportunity? How did they determine that this market was moving toward commodity status with declining margins? And how did they uncover a new opportunity to become the one place for independent investors to go for investment information and tools? Not by luck. Instead, Schwab systematically revisits their business and the markets they serve and proactively sets a future direction, well before the bottom falls out of their current business. How did Hewitt recognize that their traditional human resources (HR) consulting market was becoming commodified and their position undifferentiated? How did they manage to leapfrog their traditional competitors to become the largest provider of outsourced HR administrative services, such as benefits administration services? How have they found ways to marry their consulting and outsourcing expertise to create unique, valued solutions for clients that Hewitt's competitors cannot touch? Hewitt recognized the challenges facing their current business, uncovered the emerging opportunity for HR outsourcing, prioritized resources, and stood firm while investing heavily for several years with only modest returns. They recognized the tremendous long-term opportunity in HR outsourcing and aggressively pursued it, whereas most competitors either came late due to lack of market focus or left early due to an unwillingness to prioritize investments and ride out a few bumpy years.

Conclusion

While many service companies gain an advantage for a window of time, few are able to maintain it. Activating and executing the five market-driven processes in this chapter can help service market leaders sustain their leadership position over the long haul.

CHAPTER 13

Elevate the Role of Marketing

IN MANY SERVICE COMPANIES, THE MARKETING function has been relegated to a minor, tactical role. It is strictly an afterthought, not a strategic driver of company growth. The real drivers of the organization are operations, finance, or sales, and decisions are made through one of these three lenses. A close look at the company organization chart will show you marketing's primary focus is on tactical activities such as advertising, public relations, customer satisfaction measurement, and investor relations. While all of these activities are important, none are broad enough to have real influence over the company's direction or growth. A good example of tactical marketing organizations are service industries going through deregulation. After all, who needs marketing if customers have historically had little, if any, choice?

In reality, the marketing function should be the driving force for growth in service companies. It needs to:

- represent the voice of the customer throughout the organization
- lead the charge toward a focus on markets and customers for every function in the organization

- lead, influence, and integrate the growth initiatives across the organization—including initiatives focused on operations, sales, customer service, human resources, and technology
- drive the long-term planning process

The marketing function needs to be viewed differently from how it has been traditionally viewed—not as a tactical, support function but rather as a strategic marketing function. Fundamentally, the input required for making most strategic decisions should be customer- and competitor-driven. If a strategic marketing function is focused on the long-term growth prospects in each market the company serves, it constantly takes the pulse of the market trends, competitive dynamics, customer needs, and internal capabilities to determine where and how the company should act. In this way, a strategic marketing function is positioned to direct the company toward high-potential, longer-term growth opportunities.

A large commercial bank attempting to elevate the role of marketing ran into roadblocks from multiple directions. Historically, sales, operations, and information technology functions drove the company's decision-making process. After completing a large merger, the company attempted to establish a stronger marketing orientation. However, the organization's old "muscle memory" for making decisions continued to prevail.

- First, the company needed to move all customers to a standardized, new technology platform so as to increase operational efficiency and reduce support requirements. While this seemed like a great opportunity to use customer and market input prior to spending millions of dollars, the operations function felt it knew what was best for customers. The marketing function was unable to have an impact on the design of the new platform, not even on the design of the customer interface or the approach to moving customers from the old platform to the new one. The result was a suboptimal design of and a bumpy transition to the new platform—with many lost customers along the way.
- Second, the marketing function wanted to treat segments of customers differently in terms of products offered, pricing, service levels, and sales support. However, the "Relationship Managers" really owned the customers, and these managers were not willing to con-

sider an approach that managed each customer segment in a different way. As a result, the company ended up spending too much time with low-value, price-sensitive customers, and too little time with high-potential, partnership-oriented clients. In the end, profitability and customer retention suffered.

• Finally, the marketing function hoped to keep the company ahead of competition by being a driver of new product development. However, the information technology organization took responsibility for the majority of all product development activities and maintained a territorial approach to these activities. Marketing was not included as a core team member on development teams. Consequently, no one consistently focused on bringing the pulse of the market into new-product development projects. The bank's track record for new-product launches has been predictable: competitors frequently beat them to market, and the bank continues to launch new products that do not effectively address customer needs.

This example illustrates the real challenges companies face in trying to elevate marketing's role in a service company.

Marketing's Extended Influence

Where does a strategic marketing function need to influence the business? In service companies, marketing needs to influence almost every aspect of the company from the top down and the bottom up. Clearly, any point of contact with customers needs involvement from marketing. And its influence should include at least the following non-marketing functions (see Figure 13.1, page 212):

• The human resources function—for selecting, training, and compensating employees, particularly customer-contact employees as well as other employees responsible for delivering on company promises. In particular, marketing must help determine the profile for customer-contact employees so that this profile reinforces the company's unique competitive positioning in the market (as discussed in Chapter 12 under the "People Adoption Process"). Service companies need to attract and hire customer-contact employees that fit their unique model for success.

Figure 13.1 **Marketing's Influence on the Business**

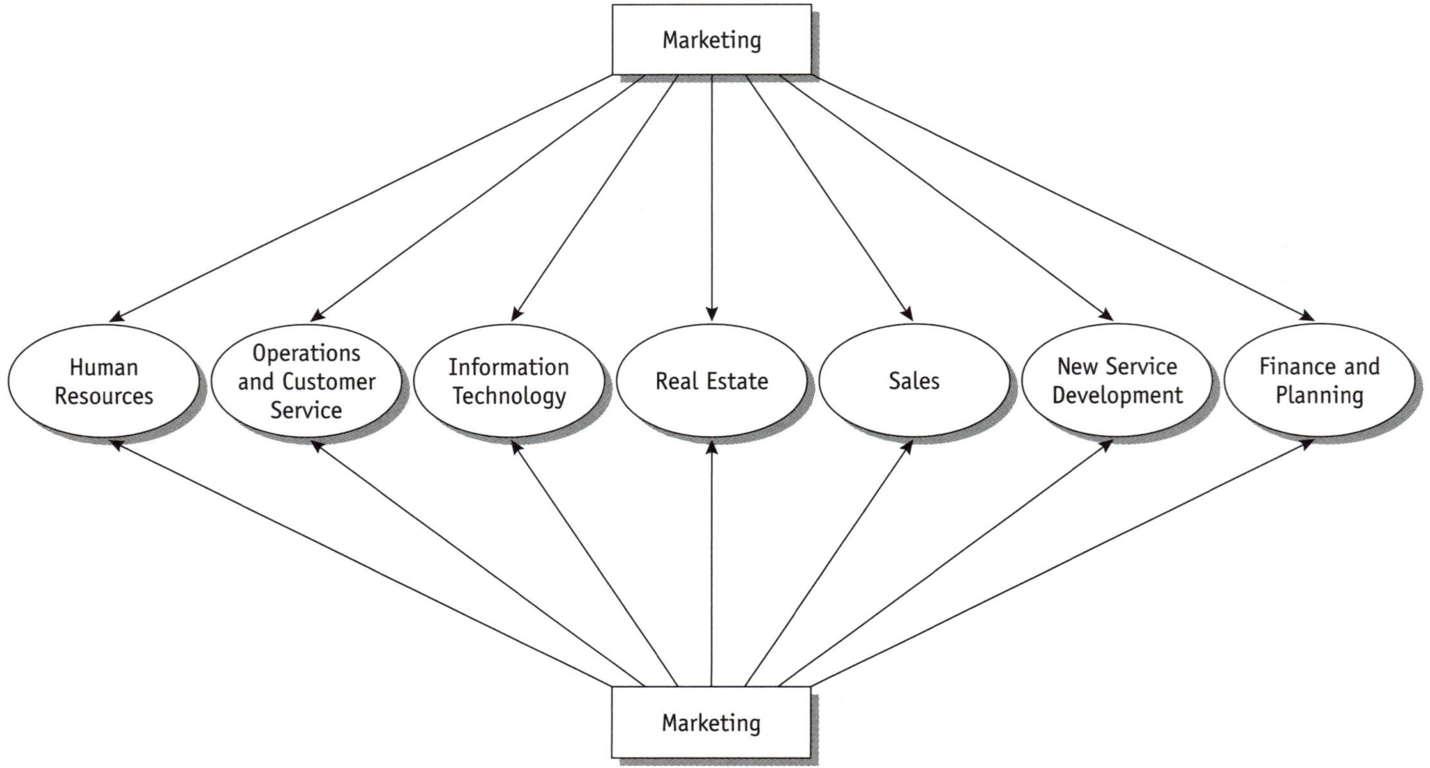

Marketing

Human Resources

Operations and Customer Service

Information Technology

Real Estate

Sales

New Service Development

Finance and Planning

Marketing

• The operations (service delivery) and customer support functions—for developing customer service procedures and service recovery processes. How much latitude should customer-contact employees have in addressing unique customer needs and handling customer complaints or problems in the event of a service failure or breakdown? How do employees balance treating customers fairly, responding quickly to unique situations, and not giving away too much to customers whose complaints are not justified? Marketing should help establish the policies and procedures surrounding these critical issues.

• The information technology function—for designing customer-technology interfaces as well as systems that support customer-contact employees. One automotive repair retailer installed an expensive new store system only to find out later the system dramatically slowed the customer check-in and checkout processes. Customers were unhappy with the long wait times, and employees were frustrated when the new system did not help them do their jobs. Until the system design and responsiveness was improved, employees worked around the system—handling paperwork manually during the day and entering orders into the system afterward. The computers served as expensive paper-weights at the front counters of each store. Marketing should play a role in helping design and evaluate any equipment or technology that directly interfaces with customers or customer-contact employees.

• The real estate function—for designing facilities, layouts, and signage. Do the facilities reinforce the desired brand image? Do facility layouts support how customers want to buy services and receive services? The tangible items customers see and react to from the company (e.g., stores, trucks, uniforms) impact their perceptions of it. How many times do customers walk into a store with such poor signage that they can not find what they are looking for? Marketing should influence the design of facilities and the tangible messages sent out to its customers.

• The sales function—for determining sales approaches, promises, training, measurements, and compensation. How much pricing authority should salespeople have? What promises can they make about service delivery? How should salespeople be measured? McKinsey, arguably the world's leading management consulting firm, recently made a major change in how it measures and compensates partners (i.e., its sales force). Sales volume is no longer the primary metric for partners. Instead, partners are measured and compensated based on the positive results they generate for their clients' businesses. Partners simply are not rewarded for selling projects that do not produce tangible results for the client and, therefore, are discouraged from pursuing projects and clients that have a low likelihood of successful implementation. Decisions about the sales function's role in supporting the company's competitive positioning should be directly influenced by marketing.

• The new product and service development function—for identifying unmet customer needs and developing new or enhanced services to address those needs. Too often, product and service development is disconnected from the marketplace. Perhaps the information technology department, sales, or operations are the primary drivers. Over the years, best-practices research in product and service development consistently gives a clear message—early and ongoing customer involvement in the process results in higher new product and service success rates, as well as products and services that beat competitors to market. Companies should turn to their marketing function to bring the voice of the customer into the new product and service development function.

• The finance and strategic planning functions—for developing and prioritizing growth initiatives. Where should the company focus its resources? What initiatives should have the highest priority? What expectations for growth should the company have? Marketing has the most direct link to customers and competitors, and should be responsible for bringing the market perspective into strategic decisions.

Making It Happen

In service companies, marketing's influence needs to be pervasive. But it needs company-wide *influence*, not lots of people in a marketing department. At the heart of marketing's ability to influence the organization are four levers:

1. The ability to develop strong relationships and keep lines of communication open with functional executives throughout the organization
2. The use of cross-functional teams with marketing's involvement or leadership
3. Marketing's ownership of the long-term planning process, so opportunities are prioritized based on market dynamics
4. Appropriate CEO involvement in and ownership of specific marketing strategies

Building Strong Relationships Through Communications

The ability to develop strong cross-functional executive relationships and foster open communications is a "must-have" for the marketing function. As previously mentioned, a strategic marketing function needs to impact a wide range of company processes—everything from employee selection to customer service procedures. In addition, specific processes that require marketing input were outlined in Chapter 12. However, a successful strategic marketing leader needs more than just process skills. That person needs relationship-building and communication skills. How else can he or she make things happen when only a small percentage of company employees are direct reports? The strategic marketing leader must expand his or her influence through working closely with other executives in the organization. Examining successful marketing executives in service organizations, the message is a consistent one—these individuals maintain frequent, open communications across all functional areas of the company. They develop strong, lasting relationships with cross-functional leaders in the organization.

Using Cross-Functional Teams

A second lever for extending marketing's influence on the organization is the use of cross-functional teams where marketing leads or is at least involved with the teams. A marketing organization trying to impact all seven of the previously listed areas would have to be huge. Such an organization is not possible for most service companies, particularly for companies that have not valued marketing in the past.

The only way marketing can create and sustain broad influence in a company is to extend marketing's reach by participating as team members on the key initiatives of other internal groups. Marketing should find the company's top priorities that require input from the marketplace, and staff a marketing team member part-time on these teams. The teams will probably welcome an added resource. If not, marketing should put their persuasive skills to work and convince the team leader and his or her manager of the benefits that can be reaped if market input is properly incorporated and acted upon—and the risks if it is not!

Extending marketing's reach through participating on key cross-functional teams requires a different skill set among the marketing troops. A typical command-and-control skill set and mind-set simply will not work. Other team members will be turned off and will shut out the marketing representative's input. The cross-functional representatives from marketing need to master the skills of influence—such as team-building, motivating others, frequently communicating upward and outward, delivering feedback, providing positive reinforcement and recognition, facilitating meetings, persuading others, planning, and coaching.

Owning the Long-Term Planning Process

A third way marketing can influence the organization is by leading and driving the long-term planning process. In this way, marketing becomes the integrating force behind all the company's growth efforts (see Figure 13.2, page 217).

Through the long-term planning process, companies determine the importance of, strategies for, and resource commitment to key growth alternatives, including:

- Retention of existing customers
- Acquisition of new customers
- Pursuit of new markets
- Pursuit of new geographic areas
- Development of new products and services
- Revitalization of existing products and services
- Acquisition of, or mergers with, other companies

Figure 13.2 **Integrating the Company's Growth Efforts**

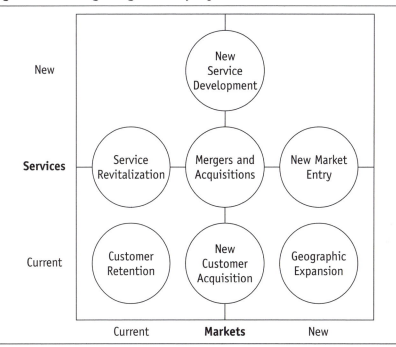

As outlined in Chapter 12, the primary objectives of the long-term planning process are: (1) to determine company strategy and competitive positioning, (2) to develop strategies for pursuing each market, (3) to prioritize growth opportunities, and (4) to allocate company resources. Marketing's role is to ensure that these four objectives start with the market—i.e., customer needs; competitor positionings and strategies; and industry, environmental, and technology trends. All the time, companies boldly and publicly claim an aggressive growth objective in order to appease stockholders and analysts, but have no plans to get there. Many companies maintained solid earnings growth in the 1990s through reengineering efforts. But then what? How will these same companies grow earnings after all of the cost efficiencies have been wrung out? And what about the employees? How do they feel about their company promising aggressive growth when there is no track record of true growth and no real idea of how the goals will be achieved? Employees have to piece together the puzzle on their own and figure out how company growth goals can be met.

Executing an effective long-term planning process is the first step toward getting back on a growth path. And because the best long-term plans are solidly grounded in the marketplace, marketing is best suited to lead this effort.

Getting CEO Involvement and Ownership

Finally, the CEO can spread marketing's influence throughout the company. But growth has to first be recognized throughout the company as a top initiative. And, if the company really wants to be a market leader, the CEO must be actively involved in paving the way for market-driven growth. Think about Dave Thomas from Wendy's. We have seen him on TV commercials for years touting Wendy's unique points of difference. He has become a vocal figure—to the public and to his employees—and he is an incredibly supportive spokesperson for the company's brand as well as its dedication to customers.

Marketing has to let go of some things and push them up. Do not delegate down or over, but get it on the CEO's plate. What should marketing push up?

• The CEO should articulate the mission and longer-term company vision. The mission articulates *why* the company is in business, and the vision describes *who* the company wants to become and *how* growth is a primary initiative in achieving the vision. Employees need to hear the overall company mission and vision directly from the CEO over and over again. Delivered by anyone else, it would lose credibility. Left unsaid, the organization will drift and lose focus. Push this one up to the CEO.

• The CEO should take responsibility for the brand. The brand is what the company stands for in the minds of customers and employees. Who owns the brand at Schwab? At Southwest? There is no doubt—the chairman/CEO. Ask your CEO if he or she thinks about the brand, worries about the brand, or is involved in shaping the brand. If not, then you do not have their ownership yet. Get your CEO involved in setting the brand strategy, ensuring priorities are aligned to deliver against the brand's promises, and monitoring the brand's value. Chapter 6 described the details. Get the CEO to read it, then push this one up.

• Demonstration of a customer-first service culture. This requires active involvement with customers and frontline employees. Why does Bill Marriott visit approximately 85 percent of all Marriott hotels in a given year? Why does McDonald's close down corporate headquarters every year and have all employees work in a McDonald's restaurant? They are *living* a customer-first culture, where all employees are encouraged to be in direct contact with customers. They are demonstrating to customer-contact employees that these employees are essential to the company's success. After all, if you are not serving customers or helping someone who is serving customers, then what are you doing? What else is a service company all about except for customers and the employees that serve them? The CEO must live this truth and personally contribute to creating a service culture. Put this initiative on the CEO's plate.

Conclusion

What does it look and feel like to be in a company where marketing's role has been elevated? Companies with a full appreciation of marketing's role can answer "Yes" to most of the questions below. Can yours? (See Figure 13.3.)

Figure 13.3 **Marketing Influence Quiz**

1. Does the company spend more time talking about customers and competitors than it does about the internal organization and politics?
2. Do most people in the organization interact every day with either customers or people who directly serve customers?
3. Is marketing represented on most key internal initiatives?
4. Is marketing driving the strategic planning function?
5. Does the CEO seek input from marketing leaders on critical decisions?
6. Does marketing encompass more strategic functions than just PR, advertising and research?
7. Do employees view marketing as an attractive long-term career path?
8. Do the CEO and senior management team meet regularly with customers?
9. Are growth and innovation integral parts of the company vision?
10. Do most employees understand the desired brand identity and how they personally support it?

Scoring: Give yourself a 1 if you answered "Yes" and a 0 if you answered "No." Then score yourself:

8–10: You are there. Marketing has been woven into the fabric of the company and is a key driver of future growth. Call us and we will use you as an example in the next edition of this book.

5–7: You are on the right track. Identify and concentrate on a few areas from this chapter where you feel progress is still needed.

Below 5: It's time to focus on changing the mind-set and elevating the role of marketing, or find a new employer!

CHAPTER 14

Redefine the Franchise

ALL SERVICE LEADERS MUST COPE WITH THE evolving commodification of their industries. The speed with which this happens varies from industry to industry—slow in the case of regulated and stable industries to extremely fast for emerging industries. Successful service market leaders redefine their customer franchise and the core benefits they provide to customers before competitors do—simple, unarguable observation. The real quandary comes in the details: When do you redefine? Where do you take the organization next? What new value should you provide?

By 1995, the commercialization of the Internet was fully under way. One early leader had emerged to help nontechnical types more easily find specific information from the vast sources of information located on the Internet. The service company is Yahoo! In the beginning, Yahoo! defined itself as a search engine, which is akin to an electronic card catalog for the Internet global library. The major benefits to customers were simpler access and easier navigation to Web sites that contained the desired information based on topic searches. Within twenty-four months of inventing their category in their emerging industry, Yahoo! had more than five strong competitors. From a customer's perspective, their search engine was no different than any others'. Lack of customer loyalty became a critical issue. The time had come to redefine the franchise. Yahoo! moved from being a service that searches Web sites to being a service that provides on-line information and resources. It also moved to capture the large, growing customer segment of people less inclined to seek out individual Web sites themselves, but rather more interested in a one-stop shop service that they would go to first. Yahoo! further ingrained this customer behavior by offering personalization capabilities through My Yahoo! that made it even more convenient to stay with one provider. By 1998, Yahoo! had successfully redefined their franchise to be a portal, a window to the vast sea of on-line information and resources. With the pace of change on the Internet, Yahoo! will soon need to redefine the franchise again.

This chapter discusses the need for service companies to redefine the value and benefits provided to customers once parity is reached among the major competitors. This can be done through repositioning the entire business, refocusing on a market niche and customer segments, or reinventing the entire service experience being offered to customers. No matter what the specific answer, service companies must always be sensitive to determining *when* to redefine their franchise because of the nature of fast-commodifying service markets.

Redefining a New Benefit to Offer Customers

An example of a company that redefined the benefit it offers to customers is Information Resources Inc. (IRI). As mentioned earlier, IRI is the world's second-largest research company for collecting consumer scanner data captured at retail stores, and then creating consumer behavior reports and other strategic market information for product manufacturers. In the early 1990s, IRI was embroiled in a severe price war with its main competitor, A.C. Nielsen. Both competitors were positioned as "collectors and deliverers of market data" and had many established clients. While IRI's market share was holding its own at more than 60 percent, the cost to maintain that share was being paid for with declining prices. The market niche seemed to be fully matured, as indicated by slow growth and falling margins. While non–U.S. clients were viewed as the new area for growth, both competitors were struggling to profitably capture this opportunity, given the high levels of investments required and the multiyear selling and relationship-building cycles.

By the mid-1990s, IRI was locked into a multiyear price battle with their rival A.C. Nielsen. This battle had paralyzed IRI's innovation spirit. It was also taking its toll on employees. In fact, cost cutting and short-term competitive battles were occupying the majority of every manager's time. Clients were demanding lower prices for what they perceived to be standard services. The prior few years, IRI had spent a fortune on its innovation-oriented heritage by pursuing a product-innovator positioning and creating lots of new products. But revenue growth was not occurring at the desired profit margins. IRI had many very loyal clients who valued the many new ideas and product innovations provided by IRI as well as their working relationships with the people at IRI. In the past, clients could always justify IRI's premium price paid versus what was generally believed to be A.C. Nielsen's price. However, as parity perceptions crept in, senior management at IRI's client companies began expressing their doubts about the high price of "just research reports to tell us what we already are doing."

Through customer research, IRI management learned a startling fact: customers use less than 30 percent of the information provided. It's no wonder they wanted a price break. Because of IRI's people and innovations, their real value-added was in the other 70 percent of the information provided that was *not* being used. In addition, Nielsen could not easily match IRI's capabilities in this arena. For years, IRI had been creating new benefits for clients in the form of new technologies and products, but not helping clients to realize the benefits. And since clients were not taking full advantage of IRI's leading-edge offerings, Nielsen had been able to maintain parity by copying their basic innovations (as a fast follower) and then offering a lower price since Nielsen didn't have the research investments to make.

Thus, IRI management decided to differentiate from Nielsen by going after the 70 percent of value the clients were not realizing and that Nielsen couldn't easily produce. This would allow IRI to grow the overall market niche, since more dollars would be spent in total. In addition, IRI would be viewed as the "integrated innovator" with clients, whereas Nielsen would be viewed as the "base service, low price" provider to clients. While there were segments of clients who preferred one approach or the other, management believed that a significant number could be convinced, over time, to do more strategic decision making with the information IRI offered.

The solution involved coming up with new ways of interacting with clients. IRI's new approach would include developing, with each client organization, multiple levels of relationships and creating a delivery capability that could analyze and determine how a specific client could make more strategic market decisions utilizing the information and expertise of IRI data and people. This new capability featured mass data collection and analysis coupled with customized information and integration.

IRI's results have been impressive: increasing margins, new competitive wins, and the continuation (versus abandonment) of an innovative corporate culture. Within a few years, IRI has recaptured its edge. They deliver new ideas, technologies, and solutions that make their clients more competitive by increasing clients' usage of market-based information for making strategic decisions. IRI dared to strategically innovate what benefits they offer and how they deliver those benefits.

Was it time for IRI to redefine the niche or move to a different business area? Neither; they just needed to redefine the benefits being delivered. Management had always believed in the power of innovation and the importance of defining and then satisfying the new unknown needs of their clients. But what was missing? It was the strategic innovation of the fundamental promise IRI was making to its clients. IRI's platform to differentiate did not work anymore.

IRI innovated the strategic elements of their service. They redefined their promise to clients by adding process innovation to the mix. Previously, IRI's promise was, "we'll package up our data and deliver it to you in the most convenient, easy-to-use, easy-to-understand, preanalyzed, customized, sliced-and-diced data format we can possibly create." This promise featured an efficiency theme in the delivery of data, with an arm's-length approach to effectively using the data. Now the promise is "we'll work closely with you to help you see, understand, and use the strategic capabilities of the information we gather from the field. Our information will become your executive decision-making system." IRI's information services now help clients use information as a strategic weapon for their future strategic and competitive decisions, versus accessing data as a tactical measuring tool for past activities.

IRI implemented their new positioning through a new sales approach as well as through new process innovations to change the behavior of clients. IRI also targeted clients who desired a close working relationship.

The new platform was actually a growth objective—in essence, grow the market niche by going after the "other 70 percent" described earlier. Nielsen had decided to follow a low-cost producer objective. Thus, IRI decided that winning was about being different from Nielsen by creating service experience innovations and not trying to do the same things better and cheaper. It broke the cycle of low growth and low profitability by promising a new type of value and benefit to its clients.

Creating New Value

Somewhere along the way, service companies seem to have stopped producing real value for their customers. This is not to say that they have produced no value or no innovations. The problem is that they mostly create *tactical* value or value with a little *v*—new features, extensions of current offerings, quality approaching no defects, skilled people at the point of interface with customers, and new marketing programs. What brings in many new, loyal and high-paying customers is *strategic* value or value with a big *V* that is the big victory over customers' perceptions of parity among providers.

The challenge lies in a service company's ability to translate the business goals and objectives into market leadership and growth-producing strategies. To be effective and easily understood, these strategies should be displayed on one page. Figure 14.1 (page 226) is such a page of one market leader—Kinko's. It shows how the externally oriented strategies of strategic benefit and unique advantages blend together with the definition of the business. It is these externally oriented strategies that form the foundation for market leadership and growth. In addition, Figure 14.1 shows how Kinko's, as a true innovation service leader, has redefined their previously successful strategies.

Figure 14.1 **Kinko's Market Leadership Strategies**

KINKO'S

Original

Business Definition:	Retail Copy Center Services
Target Customers:	Small Office/Home Professionals
Customer Benefit:	"Your Branch Office"
Unique Advantage:	24-hour store access to complete array of traditional large company office support services

Market Leadership Vision

Business Definition:	Direct Business Support Services
Target Customers:	Mobile & Independent Professionals
Customer Benefit:	"A New Way to Office"
Unique Advantage:	Multiple ways of 24-hour access to complete array of state-of-the-art business support services

Service market leaders know about risks. It is the rare business that incorporates risk-taking into their long-range plans, let alone drives the business by it. Growing a business as the market leader, however, requires taking risks. The growth direction and types of innovations can be ascertained, but the outcomes are fuzzy and the path to get there is uncharted. What is needed is a belief that a more glorious future awaits the company. What is also needed is a belief that the company will provide a set of benefits that will uniquely produce value to customers. In both cases, a leap of faith (and an acceptance of long-term risk) regarding how the company will get there is essential.

Sprint is an innovative organization that thrives on taking risks and creating value. They have grown to be more than a $10 billion service organization. A decade earlier, investing in and building a fiber optics network seemed absurd to many competitors, but has proved to be a significant source of unique benefits for customers. Similarly, the bold strategy to transition its corporate identity in the marketplace from United Telecom to Sprint has produced significant brand equity for the company.

Senior management at Sprint has repeatedly shown an interest in future possibilities and an uncanny ability to envision the future from a customer's viewpoint. This was put to the test as the 1990s found Sprint once again mired in intense competition with a half dozen strong global competitors. Management set a course to produce integrated benefits for customers across services, technologies, and physical boundaries, which required looking beyond the potentially debilitating limitations of regulations, scale, global capacity, and local connection to homes. As the years unfold, these limitations are being addressed either through persistence or just good fortune. In 1994, management once again was taking risks. This time they used a new form of wireless communications and investments that would eventually require several billion dollars in licenses and infrastructure development. Recently, Sprint announced their intention to be the first major long-distance provider to reinvent their telecommunications infrastructure and take advantage of new technology that delivers new customer benefits—once again.

The drive to provide integrated benefits for customers remains the same. It is a drive to produce a service experience that enables customers to use one communications device unfettered by physical location. It is also a drive to deliver this experience differently from competitors through next-generation technology and through industry-bridging partnerships with cable companies. Sprint is an organization predisposed to taking risks and leaps of faith in search of new strategic benefits to offer future customers.

Defining Future Benefits for Future Customers

A different direction to the New World is what made Christopher Columbus successful—not a bigger expedition, nor a faster vessel, nor a more efficient route. A different investor is what enabled Charles Schwab to create discount brokerage and become a dominant firm in the stock brokerage industry—not better reporting, nor faster trade clearing, nor massive information technology investments. A different experience is what Southwest Airlines offers, which has consistently produced profits throughout the 1990s—not better airplanes, nor faster flying times, nor the best reservation service. A different definition is what drove dramatic market share gains for UNI Insurance (one of Europe's dominant insurance companies) when it defined the customer transactions as the focus of its business and not production of better standard insurance products.

In each of these situations, the service organization defined *different* based on the future core benefits desired from its future customers. Service market leaders describe their direction for the future with a "benefits definition." This does not replace the need for a clear and unique business definition. Rather a benefits definition sets up a direction for the organization based on the intangible experience customers will value in the future. A typical business definition establishes "what we do as an organization," whereas a benefits definition establishes "the value we provide to our customers." Figure 14.2 offers examples of these two complementary definitions for service organizations.

Direction setting for a service organization must enable it to serve customers differently, not just better, than anyone else. And *different* means:

- the unique benefits customers derive from the service
- the mix of new services
- proprietary technologies
- service process changes
- unique delivery experiences
- employees' impact that enables the unique benefits to be delivered

Figure 14.2 **Business Definition vs. Benefits Definition**

	Business Definition *What We Do as* *an Organization*	Benefits Definition *The Value We Provide* *to Our Customers*
Schwab	Discount broker	Speed and effectiveness for sophisticated investor
FedEx	Package transportation	On-time package delivery and logistics management.
IRI	Research data delivery	Customer information for strategic decision making
CCC	Insurance software/ network management	Efficient claims procedure for customer impact
Columbus	New world explorer	Direct routes to the West and the Americas

Defining what future (different) benefits customers will desire from a company should come before determining how to deliver those desired benefits.

So what can be learned from successful service companies about discovering customers' future desired benefits? Successful service companies are like explorers. Simply stated, they have a willingness to move in a direction, the destination of which will not be fully defined until they get there. They use their right brain to play the "What might be possible?" association games. They save the left brain for the "What is probable?" analysis to document the business case and plan. They think and create first, plan second. They recognize their limitations as futurists and are not so arrogant as to believe they are clairvoyants. Successful service explorers have the uncanny, intuitive ability to tune into and take advantage of the macro trends and unchanging truths of their competitive service markets. These "be different" explorers can feel new market opportunities emerging over their current horizons. And they exhibit enviable ease as they define and begin moving toward new strategic destinations. Their destinations are, in fact, captured in their externally derived future benefits definitions.

Finding New Competitive Space

So how do companies discover a unique niche of benefits for themselves? Remember, like the explorers of old, you must look beyond the horizon. Unfortunately, most service companies aim only for what they see and know. Usually, this kind of vision occurs in a two-hour session in November in which management focuses on a destination that is already visible on the horizon—and, by the way, one that competitors also see. What management actually needs is a description or picture—either with words, images, or metaphors—of a uniquely defined set of benefits desired by customers at some point in the future.

Consider the benefits definition for a specific service industry: residential real estate brokerage. While highly competitive—there's a real estate company represented on practically every corner of every town—it is amazing that the vast majority do the exact same thing.

Most real estate brokerages have all clung to the industry's ancient business definition: administering the arduous process between buyer and seller. Everyone knows the drill: if you want to sell your house, you engage a sales agent who uses the Multiple Listing Service, newspaper ads, and open houses. You endure negotiations, sign endless pieces of paper, and pay a 6 percent commission. If you want to buy a house, the drill is nearly the same. The residential real estate brokerage benefits definition today could be described as "handling this frustrating process for buyer and seller so they don't have to." Gone are the days when applying expertise to manage this complex process is actually valued by customers. The industry has systematically kept the buyer both from the seller and at a controllable "arm's-length" distance from the process. This service industry is stuck in a time warp. Even with the emergence of buyer's agents and electronic self-searching, the generic real estate process seldom gets challenged. Competitors try to be different based on tactical activities such as better office locations, new pricing incentives, and more aggressive salespeople. The result has been a slow decline in industry profitability and stagnant industry growth.

So what should a company do? Apply a big dose of market leadership strategies for service companies, beginning with developing a new and unique benefits definition. And where should a new vision of the future be grounded? In identifying opportunities based on the macro trends impacting home owners (such as the increasing usage of the Internet as an interactive electronic clearinghouse), and by challenging the industry's process (such as helping both buyer and seller become much more involved in the process).

If you were the president of a large residential real estate company, what would you do? Suppose you've reengineered the corporate office, trimmed the field office management function, and downsized the number of sales agents, but are still experiencing low profitability and slow growth. What future benefits definition might you establish that would be a directional compass for your organization? Based simply on the one macro trend and one process change cited above, you could explore one daring direction: articulating your benefits definition as "control and convenience for customers through their increased involvement." Your business definition could also be modified to "an electronic residential property clearinghouse." Combining the two definitions, customers would expect to see you offering services to facilitate the transactions, such as statistical information on properties, interactive video research tools, software for maximizing your effectiveness with the personal computer and the Internet, and streamlined paperwork to speed up transaction closure.

Seeing Over the Horizon

In the late 1400s, Christopher Columbus strategically innovated within his industry—exploration—by heading west, instead of east, to reach the New World. He believed the new benefits of this direction, such as time and safety, would ultimately yield greater results for his expedition. But beyond intuitively knowing or feeling there were benefits out there, how did Christopher Columbus plot a more definitive course to discover new lands? His predicament is analogous to service organizations trying to find their way to a new benefits definition—a.k.a., new land. The following story illustrates the approach one can take as seen through the eyes of a successful mariner.

Columbus had just finished his latest meeting with Queen Isabella's court. He burst through the door of the chart-making shop he shared with his brother Bartholomew. The two men exchanged an excited embrace. "I almost have them convinced. It must be my good looks and persuasive tongue," Columbus quipped.

"All humor aside, why do you think sailing west to the Indies is the right answer?" his brother challenged.

Columbus retorted, "Because everyone else confines themselves to what they know—I am interested in what is possible. I have faith in what I can envision." Columbus called upon his years of chart-making experience to explain more calmly. "First of all, while I cannot describe the details of our destination, for it is unknown, I am confident that the benefits of being the first to reach the Orient by a western route will bring vast rewards. Second, since the overland routes to the Indies are barred to Europeans, we must go a different way. All efforts to dramatically improve the cost and safe return of an expedition east ultimately will not be successful. Third, if the world is round like many people are now claiming, then it would be possible to circle the world from west to east."

But two questions had been nagging Bartholomew for a long time. Knowing Columbus should be prepared, he asked. "Since you cannot see beyond the horizon to plot a specific course, how will you know whether to head due west or northwest? And not knowing the precise time when your destination will appear, how will you know that a voyage is even feasible?"

Columbus appreciated his brother's skepticism and warm-heartedly replied, "Oh ye of little faith. Plotting a course west is a lot like making a chart."

"So that's why you had me rig this giant sextant!" Bartholomew exclaimed. "So we can determine a direction!" Columbus was an expert with a sextant. He believed in a sextant's ability to combine firsthand, situational information with the enduring cycles of the stars in order to chart direction.

Columbus and Bartholomew spent the week going through notes from captains, key books, and many other pieces of information Columbus had accumulated over the years. Using the sextant, they created a working model of where the more favorable lands would most likely be found. They also created a new map, based on the desired destination and star positions, that would guide Columbus once at sea. Finally, they determined distance and time, about 2,400 miles and two months at sea, to go from Spain to the Indies.

Columbus eventually won the financial backing from the monarchs of Spain, that made possible his historic voyage. He abetted his own cause by explaining his vision of new lands within time and spatial dimensions.

Similar to Columbus's navigational sextant, service organizations need a similar tool for establishing their benefits definition. The sextant is ancient technology used originally by ocean mariners to chart a direction while at sea. It does not predict the future, but provides captains with a vision of their present and potential future directions so they can build their strategies of conquest. This strategic charting device is effective because it is based on things of nature that are true and that move in predictable patterns, such as the stars and sun. In this way, the sextant can plot a course that goes beyond the visible horizon.

Developing a vision or depiction of the future benefits definition requires a "market sextant." Simply stated, the market sextant is a metaphor that describes a procedure for looking over the horizon in order to map the new areas of benefit that will lead to a new benefits definition. In order to be different from competitors, service companies can sight their market sextants on those marketplace truths and trends that will guide them into the future.

The market sextant examines trends in light of basic service market truths in order to portray the emerging definition of the market—the new service horizon. Given the vast changes wrought by new technologies, worldwide outsourcing, and massive industry restructurings, the whole notion of what constitutes a service industry or market must be continually challenged and redefined.

Using a Market Sextant

To use a market sextant, service organizations should follow four steps toward a new benefits definition that will lead to being different, and thereby more successful, than their competitors. The steps are:

1. Adopt an explorer's disposition
2. Follow a different approach to direction setting
3. Define the customer's future service experience
4. Define the new benefits customers will desire

Adopt an Explorer's Disposition

A passion for discovery is, believe it or not, something we all have. But we must coax this feeling into our consciousness in order to see beyond even the big picture. For most of us, pulling one's head up from our day-to-day work to think strategically results in merely verifying what is already known and being pursued. Explorers, however, believe that a new or different picture is emerging. They know something is out there, even though others do not see it. They become determined to discover it and then to reap the rewards that come to the initial market leaders.

An explorer's disposition is toward the future and, preferably, toward uncharted and evolving markets. Like an options trader on the exchange, new market explorers watch for fluctuations in market boundaries. With fluctuation and change come the opportunities for discovery. And it is only through discovery that service businesses can leave competitors in the dust—at least for a while.

Service markets today are only too happy to oblige. Due to deregulation, information technologies, and globalization, service markets are no longer well-defined and stable. Your service organization may already be experiencing the rapid ride toward market commodification. If you are not now, you will.

And what will you do when the competitive marketplace begins to heat up? In the past, you probably started doing things that have worked well before. You tried offering more value, but the market seemed to want only lower prices. You raised your quality to a new level, but the market greedily and unrewardingly snatched this new value. In desperation you demanded to know what the market really wanted. It told you to just do the simple things better and cheaper. You promised to do better. Then your exploration-oriented competitor came along and offered customers a new game to play. Instantly, their cries became joyful. They warmly embraced your competitor and a new leader was born. You were left wondering "Why didn't *we* come up with this new game?"

A modern-day "explorer," Charles Schwab's first expedition occurred during the early 1980s. As the brokerage industry was deregulating and the history-making bull market was gaining speed, Schwab's competitors were playing the familiar game of full service and "besting" one another with new investment products. These organizations had enough opportunities to accomplish their annual goals with the known needs of a growing investor customer base. But Schwab wanted something different. He then founded the discount brokerage market and enjoyed stunning results.

So what has Schwab been doing recently? Many copycat competitors have duplicated Schwab's discount brokerage strategies and offerings. Schwab struggles to maintain loyalty among customers while simultaneously delivering high levels of profitability. In response to this situation, senior management at Schwab has been charting a new "be different" strategy course through uncharted waters. They are trying to discover the *unknown* needs of the investor population. They appear to be creating a new marketplace between full service and discount brokerage firms. Perhaps, they will redefine what is an investor. Perhaps they will invent a new way for investors to connect directly to the financial markets via electronic media such as the Internet. While their new "be different" strategy has yet to emerge, you can count on the fact that it will. They have the passion to discover. Schwab's underlying culture (their corporate disposition) is to be perceived as different from competitors. Schwab managers can feel that another market niche is emerging and they are willing to lay a course for that undefined new area.

Follow a Different Approach to Direction Setting

"Where should we head?" The answer to this question has been central to the success of organized people since time began. Businesses add "Where should we head *to win big and make the most money?*"

The common business practice when charting a future course is to start with "Where are we now?"—today's position. Then the company builds probable scenarios as to how they might evolve from this position, given some understanding of future customer needs and the changing dynamics of the marketplace. It's a logical, left-brain approach. It works well to gain incremental market share improvements from one year to the next. It works well for repositioning product businesses in stable markets. It works well for finding niches within mass markets. It does *not* work well for directing a service business to becoming a provider that is perceived as truly different from its competitors.

There are three shortcomings in the old approach:

1. The intangible nature of a service experience calls for greater emphasis on concept and perceived value. It is difficult to chart and respond to changing customer expectations. In truth, how in the world can a company predict where expectations may be in the future? The answer lies in the fact that the

result of a service is ultimately a human feeling. The memory of the pleasure or satisfaction wanted by future customers must serve as the beacon.

2. Services tend to evolve rapidly because they are easily copied by competitors. Scenarios can limit the scope of future market opportunities because they are grounded in today's reality, versus what could happen tomorrow. The mind-set must be long-term—outside the box. A better alternative? Focusing an organization's unbridled creativity around the "what could happen" possibilities.

3. The old direction-setting approach focuses most of the attention on the known, yet unmet needs of today's customers. Plotting the future requires adding an understanding of the "unknown, so unmet" needs of tomorrow's customers. Being different usually requires market boldness in defining for customers what functionality they will want.

We would like to suggest that a new direction-setting approach be followed for moving your company to a position of being different from your competitors. It is simply this: think . . . create . . . explore . . . Spend the time and energy to develop future market definitions. Once the skeleton of these future markets is identified, then put the meat on the bones. In other words, create the "lands of opportunities" around each potential exclusive market segment. To initiate this approach, brainstorm all the possible customer types that may be interested in a particular service. Next, brainstorm all the possible benefits that may be sought by these customers, keeping your reality-check red flag in your pocket until later. Finally, test the plausibility of and interest in each "land" with potential customers. The final part of the new approach is to decide which "land mass" you will head toward and begin exploring.

For example, suppose you are the national commercial real estate brokerage firm CB Commercial Realty. Aside from some individual variations, you are perceived by your target customers to be similar to competitors. Breadth and quality of services are similar, brand identities are well ingrained, and customers can switch to your competitors easily. Price determines market share, while your internal cost structure determines your profit margin. A major dose of being different has been prescribed. Get the picture?

Following the new approach, you brainstorm three emerging market redefinitions. The first is having customers electronically searching and screening properties, and negotiating and closing deals electronically versus in-person. A second is giving customers access to in-depth expertise at every turn in the transaction, versus their being tied to one generalist agent throughout the buying process. A third is thinking of the business as continuous versus transactional. Twenty-year contracts might be pursued in which your customers look to you to satisfy their "space" needs, not their periodic real estate or physical property needs. These three emerging markets can be described in simple, generic themes from a customer's perspective: self-service, clearinghouse, outsourcing.

Now comes the fun, creative part. Who could be potential customers? Perhaps corporations with big staffs and large private investors. A brainstormed list of customer-perceived benefits for the self-service theme might include:

- Fast and convenient
- Greater customer control
- 24-hour access
- Quick financial analysis
- No limitations due to location
- Reduce broker-customer tension

This grouping of potential benefits becomes your first "land mass." Additional "lands" should be developed and exploratory research conducted to better understand the opportunity and viability of each one.

Define the Customer's Future Service Experience

Many service organizations seem to think just going through the annual planning ritual will set strategy. It does not. The "be different" strategy for the Israelites of ancient days was to reach and experience the so-called promised land. Their wandering in the wilderness was the "be better" process. While the journey or planning process is often fulfilling, it only occurs because a service organization visualizes the destination—the desired expected experience—for its customers. But be wary of the single greatest trap service strategists fall into: trying to define strategy based on the tangible aspects of the service offering. This trap results from the flawed human tendency to "productize" (make tangible) a service experience.

During the 1980s, the fast-food industry was caught in this trap. By defining its strategy as providing fast food, most organizations focused primarily on the tangibles of the food itself: variety, speed of preparation, taste, operations, process standardization, and the like. This is the strategy stuff that makes unenlightened product-minded managers really sizzle. This is also the stuff that snubs service customers and drives the industry to commodify. Why? Because we do not select establishments based on the tangibles. Unfortunately, the customers actually confuse service strategists by giving quantifiable feedback on tangibles such as cleanliness, speed from order to pickup, taste of food, and menu items. When was the last time a researcher asked you on the way out of a fast-food restaurant, "Was your experience here enjoyable? Why or why not?" A service company's strategy must be based on the service *experience* in order to encourage the targeted customers to select it. Fancy and innovative tangibles, such as ergonomic seating, triangular meat patties, or recyclable packaging may be impressive to customers, but tangibles alone will ultimately be unable to get more customers. It's that simple.

A few success stories do exist, however, about explorers breaking free from the traditional commodity fast-food mind-set. The first is McDonald's Corporation's relentless pursuit of a happy experience for kids. Kids do not go to McDonald's for the food, but because they get to do something special with Mom or Dad. It's a service adventure for them made more enjoyable because of coloring books, toys in their bag, playground equipment, and the good mood their parents are usually in. McDonald's could extend this service experience into homes through a TV cartoon kids club, complete with parent-kid games and badges for accumulated visits to selected McDonald's locations.

Another example is Taco Bell. Management decided that competing on food preparation efficiency or quality was merely a focus on "commodified" tangibles that did not encourage targeted customers to select Taco Bell. Management decided it was time to pursue a "be different" strategy. Today, Taco Bell's new strategy is a fixation on the service experience customers have upon visiting one of their restaurants. For example, the majority of Taco Bell employees now interact with customers. Previously, the majority were involved in behind-the-counter operations.

Finally, many years ago, SAS Airbus defined themselves as an airline carrier. They focused their research and strategies on the "what we do"and concluded that investing in updated aircraft equipment would allow them to be most pleasing to their customers. They were wrong and fell into an often-sprung trap for service businesses—focusing on the equipment. SAS management, wanting to justify its sizable infrastructure investments, adapted its operation and marketing strategies to the equipment. SAS management eventually changed their company to being "in the business of transporting people from one place to another in the safest and most efficient way possible." This is a much more powerful definition of a service business. The remedy to the trap that SAS fell into is to remember that service companies are in the service business. Companies should define who they are based on the service experience they envision for their target customers. SAS could even go a step further in charting a course to be different from all the other air transportation service businesses. Finding differentiators other than safety and efficiency would be a good starting point.

The key to defining the future customer's service experience in a new area is the ability to understand what the future customers will value. In most service markets, customers hold elevated expectations of service providers:

- high-quality service experience
- value realized by many throughout the organization
- multiple, single points of contact with the service provider
- full solutions to problems—not just the technical "products"
- multilocation availability of services offered
- access to providers' core competencies and know-how, such as R&D
- custom offerings and programs—not being treated as mass market

Generating a list, such as the one above, of customer requirements is absolutely necessary and usually comes from direct customer research. However, it only helps the company decide what they do. The other part of the formula is establishing and then redefining, refining, and fine-tuning "who we are." This process is the expedition.

Define the New Benefits Customers Will Desire

Now is the time to unpack the shiny new market sextant. First, develop what is in effect a map of the key points of light in the sky. Stated another way, you must apply a grid or map that has one of the axes outlining the range of potential experiences a customer may possibly encounter in your service market. These are not activities. The other axis might be the type of relationship a company has with customers (periodic, integrated, arm's-length, technological). While the expected benefits get grouped into quadrants, the potential definitions of experiences form the boundaries of the quadrants. In this way, you can address the feeling that "with all these benefits around, there must be a desired experience in there somewhere."

Consider an example of how this situation might have looked from management's perception when Southwest Airlines was founded. The first axis or continuum represents potential customer experiences:

1. greater perceived value due to low prices
2. more convenience, as flying is faster than driving
3. more fun on business trips due to entertainment provided by flight crews
4. greater personal fulfillment visiting a major city for the weekend and interacting with other passengers.

The second axis of the map represents the type of relationship between the airline and its customers. It ranges from an integrated experience in a do-it-yourself environment for Southwest to a "we'll do it all for you, even carry you on our backs if necessary" approach for American Airlines. With this crude map of the horizon, you can start to see the unique fertile land Southwest pursued. The market for air transportation is depicted on the benefits map in Figure 14.3 (page 241).

Can you articulate this type of customer experience and benefits map for your service business?

Once the key points of light and the initial dimensions of the horizon have been identified, you will be ready to seek out potential "land

Figure 14.3 **Map of Benefits for Air Transportation**

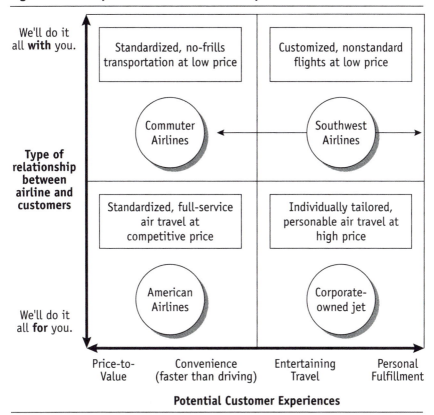

masses" or market niches. Service explorers need to envision a future and plot a course that leads to true market differentiation.

There are some traps to avoid when service companies try to reinvent ahead of their competitors, including:

- letting your company's large infrastructure dictate your strategy
- focusing too much on the tangibles of the service, when the strategy should be an expression of the experience you want for your future customers
- not realizing how quickly competitors can copy a service, so not setting strategies far enough into the future
- focusing only on the known needs, not the unknown needs, that provide the information required for breakthrough redefinition of a market

Conclusion

Leaders such as Charles Schwab, Taco Bell, and Southwest Airlines dared to be different. Each redefined the core benefits it wanted to provide for its customers and, thereby, redefined their franchises. Even Christopher Columbus sought to redefine his industry and deliver unique benefits to his customers ahead of his competitors. He had a passion for discovery, had a bold attitude about defining a new direction, understood what his "customers" (European market) would value, saw the possibilities his exploration could provide through his own "market" sextant, and surrounded himself with mates who shared his vision and commitment for the voyage. No wonder he found the New World!

CHAPTER 15

Market Leadership Strategies at Work

UP TO THIS POINT, *MARKET LEADERSHIP STRAT-egies for Service Companies* has put forth the key strategies and frameworks for creating profitable growth and achieving market leadership. It has challenged the popular growth techniques of the 1980s and 1990s by asking: "Why pursue growth through acquisition, diversification, or price maneuvers, which are fleeting at best, when you can internally create growth and be rewarded with higher margins?" It has provided countless examples of companies that are successfully applying the underlying principles of market leadership. In this chapter, we provide a comprehensive view of all the market leadership strategies at work in one company: FedEx.

FedEx is arguably one of the most successful and most innovative service market leaders of the second half of the 1900s. It pioneered an industry and built a cultural foundation that may bend to the wind of stiff competition, but will ultimately snap back to a stronger position than before. In fact, it experienced some tough times a few years ago. In the mid-1990s, management awakened to the fact that initiatives like higher-quality, reengineered operations, and economy-of-scale acquisitions were no longer delivering unique value to customers. In fact, these initiatives were at the very root of ever-intensifying price competition in the overnight package delivery industry. This concluding chapter highlights how management addressed their situation using the service market leadership strategies. FedEx's response to changing customers and a competitive environment is a powerful example of how a service company can create growth again and again.

The Symptoms of Commodification

In the mid-1990s, Federal Express (the company's name had not yet been changed to FedEx) pursued and received new insights from the marketplace and customers. The conclusions were clear. Customers did not view Federal Express to be any different than its competitors, nor were they fully aware of Federal Express's extensive geographic capabilities and scope of services. Worse yet, buyers considered overnight delivery services to be ancillary and tactical to their roles as shipping managers. Moving packages overnight had become commonplace. Customers simply expected that the transportation logistics would occur as planned. In short, Federal Express's service was no longer as valued by customers as it had been in the past. All the major competitors were providing high enough quality levels and enough new features to meet customer expectations. The management team at Federal Express was reeling from the results of severe competition. These results can be summarized in eight symptoms of commodification:

1. Low perceived expertise. Customers were no longer impressed with having things shipped overnight and delivered to practically any location. Simply stated, their fear-factor had come way down. For Federal Express, the result of this phenomenon was that customers placed less value on the overall category.

2. More diverse market. Federal Express's corporate shipping customers stopped looking like a homogeneous market. The original standardized overnight carrier service could no longer satisfy all the needs of the marketplace. Competitors were beginning to specialize on important dimensions to niches of customers. As a result, some customers assigned low value to Federal Express's service.

3. More sophisticated customers. Federal Express's corporate customers had become more sophisticated and more knowledgeable

about shipping. At the same time, they were being pressured to out-source more routine activities in hopes of lowering costs. This cost consciousness was making shipping managers increasingly difficult buyers to deal with. And senior-level buyers had divorced themselves from this routine process. The net result? Federal Express was per-forming an activity that was perceived to have little strategic value.

4. Low impact of new service introductions. Prior to their new strategic innovations, Federal Express's introductions of several new services provided little assistance in attracting sizable new corporate customers. Federal Express's offer of 10:30 A.M. guaranteed delivery, which required a significant new investment in operations, was actu-ally in response to UPS's 10:30 A.M. guarantee. Moreover, Federal Express's creation of automatic shipping and tracking software for cus-tomers was quickly copied by UPS. And their new services in Europe seemed to be forever in the shadow of DHL International. While these new offerings did help to retain most customers, there were also many customers who abandoned Federal Express to get lower prices.

5. Decreased customer share and profitability. The data seemed contradictory. Customer satisfaction ratings among Federal Express's corporate shippers had never been higher. Similarly, internal quality ratings had improved to a level even higher than when Federal Express had won the Malcolm Baldrige Award. But market share at major accounts and profitability overall was slipping. The problem was that the innovations in the industry had come in the form of "features" rather than fundamental changes to the core business. "Features" just weren't enough.

6. No longer a service organization. Federal Express went from being the expert in the early days to being a services provider, to finally being a product vendor. This last stage of being perceived as a product vendor resulted in:

- Contracts for services were bid out to many competitors.
- Long lists of criteria were developed by buyers so each provider could be compared through an "apples-to-apples" proposal.
- Price became the big factor in purchase decisions.
- The many extras, like twenty-four-hour customer service, tracking, timeliness, and convenience, were viewed as ex-pected services.

A service organization that has digressed into being perceived as a product vendor is in an ugly and unhealthy commodity position.

7. Too much standardization. In the 1990s, Federal Express was very focused on quality. Everything became standardized. Delivery drivers' jobs were routinized. Competitors, likewise, were focused on quality. Unfortunately, this high quality spilled over into customer perceptions of interchangeability among the competitors.

8. Too internally focused. Major internal initiatives, such as making sizeable investments in operations, implementing quality programs to surpass the Baldrige award quality level, and company-wide reengineering efforts had the executives in the industry focused on the nuts and bolts of running the business. Most of these executives had taken their eyes off the customers' evolving and emerging needs. The result was a less-integrated relationship with corporate customers. Customers believed that no provider truly understood their business, including Federal Express.

Taking Action

From a market perspective, management identified the market leadership opportunities that could catapult Federal Express ahead of its competition. They recognized the need to reinvent things at multiple levels and in an interrelated manner. At the most strategic level, Federal Express needed to redefine the benefits for and their identity with corporate customers. In terms of customer relationships, Federal Express needed to bring new value to individual corporate customers by integrating with them. Finally, in terms of execution, they needed to create new ways to more effectively and efficiently satisfy customers' needs.

Management started the transformation by communicating their new value-creating strategies under the banner of a new identity program. The new overall corporate strategy was to handle "any shipment anywhere, anytime, on-time." With the support of Fred Smith and other senior managers, Federal Express changed their name to FedEx and adopted a new slogan, "The World on Time." The identity program communicated the company's global scope, reliability, innovation, technology, accessibility, and speed. FedEx kept their familiar orange and purple colors to help maintain brand recognition and consistency. Communicating internally was just as crucial to successful implementation, so a diverse mix of communication vehicles were used to inform employees—from the internal newsletter, "The World Wide Update," to the internal broadcast channel, FXTV.

In addition to communications, many other market leadership strategies consistent with FedEx's three strategic goals—people, service, and profit—were implemented. Under "people," the company worked to foster healthy relationships and instill a positive attitude in the employees, reinforcing that they are integral in the process of creating and delivering innovative services. New uniforms were designed to convey that employees are friendly and accessible (different from the old uniforms that perpetuated an airline image). Regarding service, FedEx invested in redesigning everything to support the new identity—from the overnight packaging to the jet aircraft. To bolster capabilities, global expansion continued as new markets were opened in Southeast Asia. Management believed that FedEx's advantage is rooted in its strategic focus on offering a comprehensive portfolio of technology-based services. Thus, FedEx invested in research and development to create innovative new services that delivered new benefits to target customers. For example, to meet corporate customers' needs for efficiency and control, FedEx Ship Software was developed. Customers can now quickly and easily complete entire transactions from a personal computer, call for courier pickups via a modem, and print shipping labels on plain paper. Customers can track their packages on-line with a connection to FedEx's main tracking computer database.

To achieve profit goals, FedEx formed a significant number of strategic alliances. For example, the FedEx Ship Software is compatible in both IBM and Macintosh environments. From a delivery channel standpoint, FedEx also established more than seven thousand new access points across the United States through retail and shipping alliances like Kinko's, Sam's Club, Target, and independently owned and operated pack-and-mail centers. This kind of grassroots network emphasizes FedEx's goal of being accessible to all their customers and forms a cornerstone strategy to drive the business well into the next decade.

The resulting new business focus, unique identity, service enhancements, and new capabilities are a proactive illustration of FedEx's overall corporate strategy to handle "any shipment anywhere, anytime, on-time." FedEx's vision for the future is clear: to be where the action is and to meet the needs of time-definite shipments—before the competition. And continued success is predicted.

The Strategies of Market Leadership at Work

FedEx invented the category originally called "overnight mail" in which they were a carrier that delivered mostly letters to selected locations. Then the category evolved to be "overnight anything" delivered to more and more selected locations. Then new competitors came in and went after niches. For example, DHL became the "international overnight anything" carrier.

In the mid-1990s, FedEx wanted to reinvent the next dimension of the category to carve out new, more profitable competitive space as a growth platform for the next three to five years. In so doing they were willing to risk losing the brand equity they had being labelled by the generic category name of "overnight mail." What FedEx wanted to do was keep competitors in the "overnight carrier" business definition, while FedEx invented a new integrated service experience with their corporate customers. In other words, generic and product-oriented "package transportation" is now more of an enabler of this much grander, broader service called "logistics management." (See Figure 15.1, page 249.)

This future-oriented strategy will incorporate innovations such as new versions of FedEx Ship Software and new information from tracking data and logistics consulting. The essential part of the strategy is to move the relationship with FedEx, from a customer's viewpoint, from outsourced to fully integrated. The customer's overall tendency had been to give more and more of the small-package shipping function to FedEx and to become less and less involved in this perceived routine activity. Except, of course, to actively be involved in negotiating the price down. The new cry FedEx desires from their customers is "bring the experts and expertise from FedEx *into* my company."

Figure 15.1 **FedEx's Core Offering to Corporate Customers**

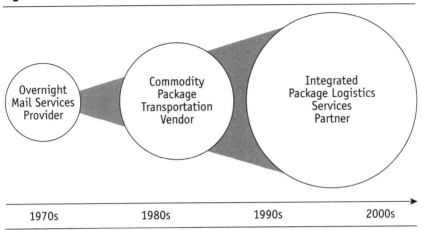

FedEx applied many market leadership strategies, although not defined this way in Memphis, that helped to reengage the company's "growth" gear. Like a car with manual transmission, companies need to shift gears from time to time as the environmental terrain changes. The decade of the 1990s, however, will be remembered as the period of time that most service companies remained stuck in the "cost reduction" and "operational efficiency" gears. When the terrain opened up new opportunities, they had difficulty finding the growth gear. FedEx employs aspects of all seven market leadership strategies for accelerated growth.

First, FedEx understands that they are a service business. They look to answer the question "What business are we in?" in terms that equate to a desired benefit or experience that customers want, not in terms that describe the kind of operations FedEx has. FedEx keeps enablers that customers don't really care about—such as new technologies and tools for efficiency—in the proper perspective. A telecommunications company that believes they are in the business of providing a global network of cable and switches, rather than providing services to help their customers communicate more effectively and efficiently, will seldom beat the competition. Likewise, if all the hotel executives in a particular city only focus on managing their physical operations better, they will create their worst nightmare—competitive parity. While competitive parity in the National Football

League may be a desirable goal, it wreaks havoc with a service company's growth and profitability.

Second, FedEx focuses on specific market niches. They don't try to be all things to all customers. Rather, they uncover and carve out profitable markets and customer segments where they can dominate. Their focus on the corporate logistics market demonstrates this commitment.

Third, they invest in creating a strong brand identity that conveys trust, along with a differentiated competitive positioning. As an organization, FedEx is obsessed with being different than competitors. The company culture takes delight in beating the competition in this way.

Fourth, FedEx thinks of innovation as a strategy—*the* strategy for future growth. CEO Fred Smith champions this mind-set. Fred Smith is a multi-dimensional man, a Renaissance man if you will. He understands the power of design and why corporate image and differentiating a company are so important. FedEx creates new services that customers value.

Fifth, FedEx understands that *how* their services are delivered is strategically important. Superior service experiences contribute to FedEx's ability to beat the competition. They therefore focus on the results of a customer's experience and the service process that the customer goes through as part of the experience. Superior service experiences are delivered in addition to the desired benefit the customer expected from FedEx in the first place.

Sixth, FedEx values and encourages the people dimension. The stories are legendary of how FedEx employees went above and beyond the call of duty to deliver packages on time. The culture and behaviors are reinforced with tangible rewards and recognition.

Finally, they have a systematic and ongoing approach for understanding changing customer needs and then inventing the new services to fulfill these needs. They also seek out new ground where they can redefine their current business to remain ahead of the commodity cycle of services.

In response to the difficult situation confronting FedEx in the early 1990s, their application of market leadership strategies is producing results. Fred Smith and the rest of the management team have indeed snapped FedEx back and have established a new market leadership platform that can drive the business well into the next decade.

Getting Started

The FedEx example illustrates the key concepts of this book. But, of course, concepts and challenges aren't enough. Business people generally want to *take action* on new ideas, rather than bask in the glow of the new idea itself.

In getting started, what is the most appropriate mind-set? A mindset that you are embarking on a market innovation crusade. It takes time to build or revive your organization's ability to invent new and valued benefits for customers. In many service companies today, developing the appropriate mind-set actually requires significant transformation, because the focus on cost cutting and reengineering has sent inventiveness into hibernation. And creation is tough and emotionally draining work.

Your market innovation crusade should nurture an approach that has the organization applying disciplined creativity to address customer needs and to take advantage of marketplace opportunities. Thus the answer is not putting the strangest and most leading-edge employees in a room until they produce a breakthrough new market innovation. The crusade should involve all those individuals who affect the demand-side of the equation in a disciplined, yet creative system of inventing new value for customers and beating competition. Discipline because the system is driven by market needs and niches—collectively determined objectives and repeatable processes. Successful creativity because the people are, therefore, focused on establishing new value for customers and beating competitors.

In working with over one hundred service companies to help them implement some or all of the market leadership strategies, the sequential framework outlined in this book has worked well in many different service companies, industries, and situations. Market leadership strategies can be divided into seven steps to facilitate implementation. Each step is linked with the others, and no one step will produce the breakthrough results desired. Rather, it is the combined effect of improving and aligning all the strategies that produces market leadership results.

Become Inventors of Growth

This book is about propelling service organizations to be dominant and enduring market leaders. It is built upon several tenets, including: a future orientation, market-derived growth opportunities, a customer-centric focus, assumed rapidly commodifying markets, innovation, organizational competitiveness, and an innovation-prone culture for individual creativity.

Service businesses have been mired in too many internally and cost-focused programs. They have pursued acquisition and diversification growth strategies only to struggle with integration into and distraction from their core business. The real challenge lies in creating *demand*, not further reducing costs. This requires significant discipline and investment in strategies for market leadership to continuously create new benefits for customers in order to drive growth. Strategic market leadership is a process that ties together all the demand-side functions and activities much like the annual budgeting process does for the cost-side elements.

While innovation and growth need to become an everyday strategy for service organizations, product companies need to begin applying the lessons learned from service leaders. This is because many product companies are using service offerings more strategically than in the past to differentiate themselves to customers. Further, many product companies find themselves capable of actually becoming service companies. All companies need to understand their best competitive opportunities and how to apply service-inspired market leadership strategies to invent growth.

Recent history in corporate America witnessed the unbridled pursuit of fast and easy growth followed by a period of "paying the piper" through painful downsizing and costly reengineering. "Get rich quick" approaches seldom work in the long term. While not as ego-gratifying as mega-acquisitions or diversification investments, managers of service companies nonetheless need to implement a more disciplined process for inventing real growth by creating new benefits for targeted customers. A company-wide mission to be the market leader invites all employees to be part of the process of creating value, serving the unique needs of customers, beating competitors, and becoming inventors of growth.

Bibliography

Berrigan, John, and Carl Finkbeinger. *Segmentation Marketing: New Methods for Capturing Business Markets.* New York: HarperBusiness, 1992.

Boyle, Denis, ed. *Strategic Service Management: Beyond the Moment of Truth.* The Best of Long-Range Planning, No. 7. New York: Pergamon Press, 1991.

Davidow, William H., and Bro Uttal. "Service Companies: Focus or Falter." *Harvard Business Review* (July–August 1989).

Drucker, Peter F. *The Practice of Management.* New York: HarperBusiness, 1993.

Green, Lee. "Out of the Gutter." *American Way* (August 15, 1998).

Griffin, Abbie. "PDMA Research on New Product Development Practices: Updating Trends and Benchmarking Best Practices." *Journal of Product Innovation Management* 14, no. 6 (November 1997).

Hagel, John, and Arthur G. Armstrong. *Net Gain: Expanding Markets Through Virtual Communities.* Cambridge, MA: Harvard Business School Publishing, 1997.

Hamel, Gary, and C. K. Prahalad. *Competing for the Future.* Cambridge, MA: Harvard Business School Publishing, 1994.

Heskett, James L. Shouldice Hospital Limited case study. Cambridge, MA: Harvard Business School Publishing, 1989.

Heskett, James L., W. Earl Sasser, and Leonard A. Schlesinger. *The Service Profit Chain: How Leading Companies Link Profit and Growth to Loyalty, Satisfaction and Value.* New York: Free Press, 1997.

———. *People, Service, Success: Mobilizing People for Breakthrough Service.* 30 min. Cambridge, MA: Harvard Business School Publishing, 1993. Videocassette.

Kotler, Philip, and Paul N. Bloom. *Marketing Professional Services.* Englewood Cliffs, NJ: Prentice-Hall, 1984.

Kuczmarski & Assoc., Inc. "Winning New Product and Service Practices for the 1990s." Kuczmarski & Assoc. (1995).

Kuczmarski, Thomas D., *Managing New Products: The Power of Innovation.* Englewood Cliffs, NJ: Prentice-Hall, 1992.

———. *Innovation: Leadership Strategies for the Competitive Edge.* Lincolnwood, IL: NTC Publishing Group, 1995.

Levitt, Theodore. *The Marketing Imagination.* New York: Free Press, 1986.

Lovelock, Christopher H. *Services Marketing.* New York: Prentice-Hall, 1996.

Lovelock, Christopher H., and George Yip. "Developing Global Strategies For Service Business." *California Management Review* 38, no. 2 (January 1996).

Pollard, C. William. *The Soul of The Firm.* New York: HarperBusiness, 1996.

Reis, Al, and Jack Trout. *The 22 Immutable Laws of Marketing: Violate Them at Your Own Risk.* New York: HarperBusiness, 1994.

Rosenau, Milton D., ed. *The PDMA Handbook of New Product Development.* New York: John Wiley & Sons, 1996.

Rust, Roland T., Anthony J. Zahorik, and Timothy L. Keiningham. *Service Marketing.* New York: Addison-Wesley, 1996.

Shostack, G. Lynn. "Service Positioning Through Structural Change." *Journal of Marketing* 51 (January 1989).

Ziethaml, Valerie A., A. Parasuraman, and Leonard L. Berry. *Delivering Quality Service: Balancing Customer Perceptions and Expectations.* New York: Free Press, 1990.

Index

THE AMERICAN MARKETING ASSOCIATION IS the world's largest and most comprehensive professional association of marketers. With more than 45,000 members, the AMA has more than 500 chapters throughout North America. The AMA sponsors twenty-five major conferences per year, covering topics ranging from the latest trends in customer satisfaction measurement to business-to-business and service marketing, attitude research and sales promotion, and publishes nine major marketing publications.